From the book:

"There's no reason to worry about another player winning 'your' royal flush by playing 'your' machine. If someone else wins on the next hand after you quit playing, the computer inside the machine determined the timing of the jackpot, not the fact that the jackpot came on the next hand displayed."

DWIGHT AND LOUISE CREVELT'S

VIDEO POKER MANIA!!

GOLLEHON BOOKS
GRAND RAPIDS, MI

Library of Congress Catalog Card Number: 91-70312

ISBN 0-914839-20-9
(International Standard Book Number)

Photo of video poker machine, courtesy of IGT, Reno, NV.

Megabucks, QuarterMania, and Nevada Nickels are trademarks of IGT.
MegaPoker and MegaKeno are trademarks of EDT.

The authors would like to thank those who shared their knowledge and experiences with us to help make this book possible, including:

The staff and management of Electronic Data Technologies

Logan Pease, Chief engineer, International Game Technology

Mary Hayes, International Sales, International Game Technology

Jay Mielstrup, slot manager, Vegas World Casino and Hotel

Several members of the Gaming Control Board and casino operators who have chosen to remain anonymous.

Special thanks to John Gollehon for his patience while we researched and wrote this book.

Contents

1. THE EVOLUTION OF VIDEO POKER........1

   The Dominance of Video Poker 3

   A Brief History 6

   Where To Play 10

2. UNDERSTANDING THE MACHINE
   AND THE GAME 17

   How the Machine Works...................20

   Types of Machines 31

   Myth-Conceptions 38

3. POKER PERCENTAGES....................49

   Tables and Calculations..................52

   Progressive Teams.......................61

   MegaPoker 73

   MegaPoker Math 75

4. STRATEGIES 77

   Three Strategies 87

   The Optimum 92

   The Royal 94

   The Conservative 96

5. MANAGING YOUR MONEY 103

6. PERKS AND PERILS 118

   AUTHORS' PROFILE 139

   BIBLIOGRAPHY 141

From the book:

"It is now deemed more 'respectable' to participate in a game of video poker than to pour money down the hungry gullet of a 'plain' slot machine. Watching the cards being dealt is more fascinating than watching fruits and bells and bars spinning around until they stop (usually on the wrong line). Making choices on the draw gives players a sensation of control and power over the outcome; they are not entirely at the machine's mercy."

From the publisher:

When we first published *Slot Machine Mania* — the Crevelt's first book — the chapter on "Superstitions" was particularly striking... and appropriate. We all know how superstitious gamblers can be.

But what was really weird was the way the numbers on the book were coming up: The book's ISBN (a book industry number) was assigned as 21-7 (the last three digits on the publisher's code). Twenty-one? Seven?

The book's "first sale" date was July 11, 1988. July? Seven? The 11th?

And to make it really uncanny, let me quote from the book's dedication page:

> *This book is dedicated to Matthew Henry Crevelt, born appropriately on April 21, 1987, weight 7 pounds 11 ounces, height 21 inches and to his mother Jean Anne Crevelt. Also, to his brother William Michael, sister Michelle Anne, and grandfather James R. Crevelt for their patience and understanding.*

I know, I know. "Coincidence," you say. And probably so. But when we decided to do a revised paperback edition a couple of years later, the ISBN prefix we were assigned was 13-6! Thirteen? *For this book!* Yes, we're keeping an eye on it, but it's doing just fine.

Video Poker Mania got its own ISBN too, of course. The digits were 20-9. Let's see... 20 is a good hand in blackjack, and 9 is perfect at baccarat. So I guess we're safe.

But what's in a number anyway? Nothing, unless it wins!

May all your numbers be winners!

But keep your fingers crossed.

— John Gollehon

CHAPTER 1

The Evolution
Of Video Poker

Man against chance. The age-old battle still wages. Man wagers his means and searches for ways to beat the odds that always favor chance. The most famous form of this struggle is now known as "gaming," the industry's new euphemism for gambling.

Gaming has been growing worldwide in the 90's and many new areas are legalizing gambling in one form or another. There are new mega-resort casinos in Atlantic City and Las Vegas, Old West casinos in South Dakota, casinos on Indian Reservations, and the return of gambling on Mississippi riverboats and cruise ships in the Gulf of Mexico. Everywhere gaming is flourishing. One common thread in this growing network of "magic carpets" is a string of slot machines beckoning with their "magic lamps" to everyone looking for a genie to grant all their fantastic wishes.

In our first book, *Slot Machine Mania,* we revealed how the slots keep edging out the table games by generating more than 50 percent of the casino's revenue at a lower cost per square foot. *In fact, the Nevada Gaming Control Board report for April 1991, revealed that 60 percent of the revenue was from slots and 47 percent of the slot revenue was from quarter machines.* For instance, in major casinos the average number of slot machines has mushroomed from a mere 500 to nearly 3,000 over the last decade.

However, with due respect to the technological revolution, industry moguls must accept the fact that the introduction of video poker is the most significant contribution to the popularity and success of slots.

The Dominance of Video Poker

Video poker and slots provide a large part of the "jack" to grow the "greenstalk" to support the giant "castles" that seem to spring up in areas where they become a legalized "recreation." No wonder the new resort builders are returning to famous fairy tales as themes for their mega-resort casinos.

Video poker combines the skill of an age-old, relatively simple game of draw poker with the ease of playing a slot machine. These games of "skill" have been gradually outnumbering ordinary slot machines in many locations. Consequently, casinos and manufacturers are finding it difficult to maintain a balance in play between the two types of machines. Larger progressive jackpots on regular slots try to compete with the new exciting varieties of video poker, but it's a losing battle.

Despite the industry's attempts to maintain the slot-video poker balance, video poker is gradually tipping the scale in its favor. This mutant progeny in its infancy and adolescence promises to overshadow its predecessors. It is no wonder, then, why *Slot Machine Mania* has given birth to *Video Poker Mania*.

As video poker mania escalates, everyone wants a piece of the action. Would-be experts try to cash in with systems to beat the machines and/or books which outline "sure-win" strategies. Mathematicians, college professors, weekend players, casino employees, and "professional" gamblers have given it their best shot. Until now, though, we haven't seen any authoritative strategies written by someone who has designed and built video poker machines. *Video Poker Mania* fills that void.

This book explains the simple math behind the machines, the percentages of payback, and the casino's hold percentages. It shows why no system can guarantee winning all the time, contrary to all the books that say, "Use this strategy and you will have a 102 or 103 percent payback." *You are plainly not going to get it!* — at least not with consistency.

Poker machines are designed to pay back a certain lesser percentage of what goes in, and — by the grace of a computer chip — they will do that. For instance, in a short term, you might put in a few coins, hit a jackpot and walk away a winner. At that given moment the machine's payback percentage is in your favor, depending on the size of the jackpot. However, the longer you play any machine, the closer it will approach its "hold" percentage, that is, the casino's win percentage. This long-term play almost always proves the percentages out and gives the house that proverbial edge. What better reason could you have to keep your playing sessions short... and hopefully, sweet.

To help you tackle this built-in edge, our book outlines three types of strategies: the Optimum Strategy, the Royal Strategy, and the Conservative Strategy.

The Royal is for high-risk, high-rolling gamblers looking only for the big jackpot.

The Conservative is for the recreational player with limited funds who wants the maximum playing time for minimum investment.

The Optimum is for the player who wants to make the machine at least pay back its built-in percentage, but, at the same time, try to tip the odds in his favor.

By contrast, the Royal and Conservative strategies increase the house hold percentage over the long term — but *might* give you better short-term results.

Most players are not aware of the type of strategy they are using and probably switch from one to another with any given hand, based on a hunch, previous hands, someone else's advice, or desperation at losing. They often play too fast without evaluating their hand according to its potential. They may know the table game of draw poker but are not familiar with the limitations or differences on the machine game. Consequently, they may make wrong choices on the hold and draw.

Video Poker Mania gives you the facts, the probabilities, and the simplified strategies. From there you may learn to play wisely, selectively, and — if you're lucky — more successfully. What our book does *not* do is give you so many calculations and statistics that only a rocket scientist could understand. It does not try to "table" all the possibilities, only the significant ones. It gives you an eagle's eye overview of the entire video poker realm, not a mountain of math and tables that would take an inchworm years to crawl over.

We warn you, however, that no one can guarantee you a big jackpot at any given session of play for either a short-term or a long-term venture. These mega-resorts aren't built on winners. But let's see if we can at least condition you to win more often and let others do the losing.

A Brief History

In the '70s, when manufacturers developed the video screen to replace reels in slot machines, they also began to apply this new technology made popular by Atari's Pong arcade game to other games of chance. Blackjack was the logical forerunner. Its rules and method of play were easily adapted to the video screen. Bally Manufacturing produced arcade games as well as slot machines, but it was Walt Fraley of Fortune Coin Company in Las Vegas who developed the first successful line of video gaming machines.

At first, players were only mildly interested in this new slot "game." The returns on blackjack, for example, could not rival the outrageously large progressive jackpots being offered on slot machines with the new video screens and their winking, blinking characters inviting players to try their luck. That was soon to change.

Meanwhile, A-1 Supply in Reno, founded by Si Redd in 1975, was also working on a poker slot machine. Recognizing the potential gold mine in video poker, Redd bought out Fortune Coin in 1979, combined it with A-1 Supply, and renamed it "Sircoma," an acronym for *SI* Redd *CO*in *MA*chines.*

Logan Pease, chief engineer at Fortune Coin and later at Sircoma and IGT, recognized the widespread appeal of poker in locations besides the casino and decided to develop a video version of the game. Casinos, manufacturers, and Gaming Board members didn't share his enthusiasm, probably because blackjack tables and players far

---

*Co-author, Dwight Crevelt worked in the engineering department of Sircoma and was instrumental in the computer programming of their video slots and video poker machines.

outnumbered poker tables and players in every
casino.

However, Pease was not deterred and put out
the first video poker machine in quarter and dollar denominations. The players were still only
mildly interested until twelve nickel machines were
placed in Sam's Town casino in Las Vegas on an
experimental basis. Casino managers, manufacturers, and the industry in general were astounded
by the results. Players were waiting in line to grab
a machine when it became available. Casino per-
sonnel were busy around the clock — selling
nickels, answering questions about the game, paying jackpots, and correcting "coin-in / time out"
problems — while players impatiently watched
and waited to push those buttons and try their
"skill" instead of "luck." (Or so they thought!)

In 1981, Redd established International Game
Technology (IGT) and moved the main manufacturing facility from Las Vegas to Reno, retaining
a sales and service facility in Las Vegas for its
many customers in Southern Nevada. An astute
businessman, Redd also entered into a unique,
five-year agreement with Bally Manufacturing.
IGT acquired *exclusive* rights to the manufacture
and sale of video machines. In return, Bally
retained exclusive rights to reel-type machines,
their largest and most successful line at that time.
By this agreement, Redd virtually eliminated any

significant competition for expansion of the video poker line.

When Atlantic City became a gambling resort in 1978, the regulations prohibited a manufacturer from supplying more than 50 percent of the machines in one casino. Because of Si Redd's former ties with Bally, Atlantic City counted IGT machines in Bally's 50-percent limitation. After considerable legal maneuvering, however, IGT finally obtained its "independence" from Bally and was able to place its own percentage of machines in Atlantic City casinos.

Since that time, other manufacturers have come and gone. Some have had limited success with their versions of video poker, but the IGT machines, with few changes to the original configuration, are still the most popular with players. After all, veteran video poker players who first learned or became "hooked" on the IGT machine do not change their habits very easily.

A few manufacturers are still vying for market share, such as: Universal (a Japanese-owned company), Games of Nevada, and Sigma Games, Inc., but their machines have not been able to equal the appeal of the IGT machines.

Bally Manufacturing's poker machines, manufactured after the agreement with IGT expired, were somewhat popular for a time but still do not have as wide appeal in many casinos as IGT's new varieties. Bally's Second Chance machine, which has had moderate success because of its unique feature, hangs on in some places, but the number and significance in the total picture are minimal.

In fact, some reports at this writing allege that Bally is trying to sell the manufacturing division of its multi-faceted operations. (Bally now owns and operates the former MGM casino/hotels in Las Vegas and Reno, and another two in Atlantic City.) Their main manufacturing plant has been in Chicago, although they recently built a new facility in Las Vegas.

Regardless of who makes them, video poker machines have become the most popular slots in Nevada. With increased exposure throughout the world, they will probably grow in popularity everywhere, at least until someone designs a new video game machine that is as fascinating and easy to play as video poker.

Where to Play

As more and more cities, states, and countries realize that gambling exists and they might as well regulate and tax it, you will have more places to go and try your luck. With each new jurisdiction you find different types of gambling legalized, and you need to choose the area that offers the most variety or the specific type of game you prefer, as well as other activities that interest you.

For example, Las Vegas has grown into a destination resort center. Most of the larger properties have expanded into vacation spots that include more activities for families as well as just gambling. Theme-oriented casino/hotels with elaborate arcades for the youngsters (of all ages) to enjoy are becoming prevalent as new casinos are built and old ones expand to keep pace. The best example is the Excalibur (owned by Circus Circus Enterprises) on the Las Vegas strip with a medieval motif and nightly show, "King Arthur's Tournament," along with strolling performers in medieval costumes and even a "friendly dragon." In the Circus Circus tradition, families love the place.

There is a veritable smorgasbord of gambling destinations available including: Indian Reservations, Mississippi Riverboats, Deadwood, SD., the whole state of Nevada, Atlantic City, Nebraska (for keno), cruise ships in the Gulf of Mexico and on the high seas, and even various new offerings in cities and countries that were once "behind the iron curtain." *Peristroika* at work?

At this writing, other states are in the process of opening up gaming in some form or another. These include: Colorado, Illinois, Mississippi, Connecticut, Washington, Louisiana and Montana — to name a few. Since Congress passed the Indian Gaming Act, many of the reservations are opening up full casinos. Besides offering bingo, keno, and the standard table games, slots and video poker are also prominent items on the gaming smorgasbord.

To give you some idea about the relative payback you can expect at the various locations — most of the slots average in the 90% to 92% payback range while the video poker averages are in the 92% to 95% range. The following table compares the average payback percentages we've discovered for the two types:

General Payback Percentages by Location

	Slots	Video Poker
Las Vegas	92–97	92–97
Reno	92–95	92–95
Atlantic City	85–90	87–92
Indian Reservations	90–92	92–95
Mississippi Riverboats	90–92	92–95
Deadwood, SD.	90–92	92–95
Moscow & Leningrad, USSR	—	92–95
Yugoslavia	90–92	92–95

The percentages found in this chart should be considered in general terms and are subject to change. They do not represent specific casinos.

As you can see, video poker is the best gamble of the two wherever you play. Note also that the percentages are relatively consistent except for one location, Atlantic City. That is also the place with the most stringent regulatory controls that we are aware of. We're not sure about the controls in communist countries.

Roger Gros, editor of *Casino Player Magazine* said that one of the goals of his magazine is to educate the public about the variety of gaming opportunities available, especially for those patronizing Atlantic City casinos because it is *not* representative of most gaming resorts.

Not only are video poker machines less attractive in Atlantic City, but so is blackjack (the table game) as many players already know. But all you have to do is witness the action in an Atlantic City casino on a typical weekend — the table games and the machines are all full to the rim — and you'll soon wonder why the casinos would even think about improving the odds for the players. Obviously, they don't have to. The players come anyhow. And they come in droves. You figure it out.

Nevada's wide-open spaces and its tourist-oriented resorts definitely have a bearing on its popularity as a gaming destination. Tourists are given the "royal" treatment. Food and lodging ranges from cheap to moderately expensive, depending on your taste — or diet — and pocket-book limitations. There are restaurants everywhere and adequate parking. Expanded airport facilities in Las Vegas keep up with the traffic of tourists looking for a "gambling" high.

Conversely, the confinement of gaming in New Jersey to Atlantic City limits its growth potential. Because of the dense population of the Eastern Seaboard and its proximity to Atlantic City, gambler's visits are relatively short. The average gambling trip to Atlantic City is four to six hours; the average trip to Las Vegas is three to four days.

On the other hand, Atlantic City's airport facilities are inadequate and cab fare to the casino is about $40. If you park a car at an Atlantic City casino it can cost $47 over a three-day weekend. Tourists must stand in line to eat, to find a table or machine to play, or go to a show. Even the lines with VIP passes for shows and restaurants are long. We wonder if there's a line in the restrooms?

All of the mega-resorts in Atlantic City put together offer approximately 8,100 hotel rooms. That is less than the seven hotels in Nevada owned by Circus Circus Enterprises alone which boasts over 11,200 hotel rooms.

As for the machines, there are fewer varieties and only a small chance of getting the one you want especially on a weekend. What are your chances of winning or going home ahead? The percentage table just about says it all.

Next to Las Vegas and Reno, the "little" town of Laughlin on the Colorado River has become the third ranking gaming town in the state. The resort town counted 3,432,057 visitors in 1990; that's a bunch for a town with only about 5,000 residents. Laughlin's work force exceeds 25,000 with 80 percent of them living across the river in Bullhead City, Arizona, which has doubled its population in the last decade.

Even though Las Vegas and the other ranking cities in Nevada are tourist oriented, the gaming establishments are learning not to ignore the local patrons. Many of the "downtown" and off-strip casinos in Las Vegas cater to the locals.

The Las Vegas Convention and Visitors Authority conducted a telephone survey of 1,000 local (Clark County) residents (population is approximately half a million) to determine how often locals gamble and what games they prefer. In her article in the *Las Vegas Sun,* Lynn Waddell reported the survey's results: About two thirds (65 percent) of those surveyed gamble occasionally. Half of those gamble at least once a week, 30 percent play once or twice a month, and 20 percent gamble four times or less a year. It was not surprising that only 33 percent gambled most often on the strip and 19 percent gambled downtown.

According to the survey, 45 percent preferred video games while 26 percent played regular slot machines. Blackjack players were a low third with only nine percent. Poker parlors and race/sports-books attracted only five percent each. Craps, bingo, and keno attracted only 3 percent each.

Of the slot and video game players, 75 percent played quarters, 21 percent played nickels, and 3 percent played dollars. Surprisingly, only 38 percent said they play maximum coins.

Not surprisingly, the survey also indicated that the longer they lived in Las Vegas the less often they gambled.

CHAPTER 2

Understanding The Machine And The Game

Video poker machines simulate the basic game of draw poker. Initially, you are dealt five cards and are allowed to discard any or all of them and draw new cards in order to try to improve your hand. The ranking of standard poker hands is shown on the next page and is the same as in the table game.

17

Rank Of Standard Poker Hands
(In Descending Value)

HAND	DESCRIPTION
ROYAL FLUSH	Only the 10, Jack, Queen, King and Ace of the same suit.
STRAIGHT FLUSH	Any five cards in consecutive value, of the same suit, such as the 2, 3, 4, 5, and 6 of diamonds.
FOUR-OF-A-KIND	Any four cards of the same value (all four cards of the four different suits) such as the 8 of hearts, diamonds, spades and clubs.
FULL HOUSE	Five cards that include a pair and three-of-a-kind, such as a pair of Kings and three 2's.
FLUSH	Any five cards of the same suit but not consecutive, such as 8, 10, Jack, King and Ace of hearts.
STRAIGHT	Any five cards in consecutive value, not of the same suit, such as 4 of clubs, 5 of hearts, 6 and 7 of spades and 8 of diamonds.
THREE-OF-A-KIND	Any three cards of the same value such as three 9's.
TWO PAIR	Two pairs of equal value cards such as two 3's and two 10's
JACKS-OR-BETTER	Any pair of Jacks, Queens, Kings or Aces.

The major difference with this game is that you are not playing against anyone but the machine. Another player can't bluff you into giving up a winning hand. You are simply trying to get the highest hand. There is no "ante" except the coins inserted to play the machine. There are no bets to call or raise to build a "pot." The pot is predetermined and never changes (except for progressives). The higher the hand, the more you win.

You can leave your "poker face" at home. You can smile, frown, or glare at the machine if you don't like the deal. We've even heard strong language. Be polite; the players around you will appreciate your courtesy just as they would at the table games. The machine won't talk back. It won't even snicker if you make a mistake.

But some machines will alert you when you have a winning hand on the deal by flashing "winner" and type of hand on the screen, or by the sound of a bell or both. Just keep your eyes and ears open for those signals. In other chapters we explain the payback percentages of the various machines and the strategies for playing them.

It should be noted that the differences in card value are of no consequence to the poker machine player (except for a single pair of jacks-or-better). For example, three 2's pay the same as three aces. As a standard poker rule, the ace may count as either high or low in making a straight (A-2-3-4-5) or a Royal (10-J-Q-K-A).

Straights do not have to be "ordered," meaning the cards appear on the screen in exact ascending or descending order. However, some casinos offer bonus payouts for an ordered Royal Flush, such as 10-J-Q-K-A. Most standard machines and progressives will pay on a Royal, or any straight, no matter how the cards are arranged. K-10-A-Q-J, in this case, is just as good as seeing them in sequence.

Be sure to check the machine you are playing to make sure you understand exactly what hands are required, and what the payouts are... especially if any bonus payouts are offered.

How The Machine Works

We keep talking about how the machine chooses the cards. But how does it do that? As we explained in *Slot Machine Mania,* these machines are microprocessor-controlled.

Microprocessors, often called "computer chips," are miniature computers which work in conjunction with other "chips" or integrated circuits (IC's) to control all parts of the machine including the lights behind the award and logo glasses, the coin meters, the payout hopper, and the selection of the cards to be displayed on the screen. One or a series of these chips contains the programmed memory that performs all these intricate functions. The computer chips are so fast and efficient that they virtually prevent cheating.

Gaming regulators check the program of every type of microprocessor-controlled machine very carefully before it is licensed. The Nevada regulators are looking even more carefully into these routines and into the background of applicants for licenses, since they discovered a now-defunct slot route operator who had been using machines with programs modified to prevent royal flushes. We won't name the company as there are several other companies that have similar names; we wouldn't want anyone to confuse them. One sad note to this story is that the programmer who reported the "gaffed" program to the gaming authorities was found murdered shortly thereafter.

The regulators check the algorithms and the method used to calculate or select the random numbers. They examine it mathematically, theoretically, and empirically to make sure the hands are dealt in a completely random and impartial manner so as not to cheat the player. An algorithm, incidentally, is a formula or sequence of instructions for a specific task. In the video poker program, it is a mathematical formula that determines how the number or combination of numbers is to be selected and translated into a specific poker hand to be displayed on the video screen.

One of the most important parts of the program is the random number generator (RNG). The microprocessor containing the program and the RNG runs continuously unless the power is cut off. Every millisecond (1/1000th of a second) the RNG selects a random number from a sequence within a given range. Most machines use a 32-bit RNG, which will generate a value anywhere between 0 and 4,294,967,296 (exponentially 2 to the 32nd), rounded off to four billion for ease of discussion. Theoretically, it should select every number from that four-billion range at least once before repeating any number, but that is not necessarily the case in the real world, only in theory. Some numbers could be chosen more than once and some almost never as in a lottery, but still be accountable to the strict laws of probability. Within that range of numbers, a specific number or combination of numbers is translated into the poker hand dealt.

All video poker machines require an external event to select the random number, usually instigated by the player. The selection process may begin at various times, depending on how the machine is programmed. It can start at the moment the first or last coin is inserted, accepted, and/or registered on the meter; at the instant the player pushes the button for "deal"; or at some other specific millisecond after one of these actions. Only the manufacturer who programs the machines knows for sure.

After the appropriate triggering action, the microprocessor begins the selection process. It accesses the RNG which determines what cards will be dealt. The mathematical formula in the program tells the RNG to select the number or group of numbers which will correspond to a specific set of cards. Sometimes the RNG is accessed several times for the combination of cards on a single hand.

If you knew at which millisecond a royal flush or other winning hand would be chosen by the RNG, you still could not systematically play the machine to deal those hands. Several factors prevent systematic play to call out a certain set of cards. First of all, it is literally impossible to know at a given millisecond what hand the RNG will choose since the choice is "pseudo-random" — meaning that there is no historically predetermined sequence of choices. Second, even if you knew the exact millisecond, your human reaction time is too slow to play the machine fast enough to freeze that hand. For instance, the average person has a 50 to 350 millisecond reaction time; mechanical and electrical delays in the machine can vary from 16 to 50 milliseconds between plays. Consequently, there are from 66 to 400 different hands that could be selected during that time over which you have no control.

So much for worrying about another player winning "your" royal flush by playing "your" machine. If someone else wins on the next hand after you quit playing, the RNG determined the timing of the jackpot, not the fact that the jackpot came on the next hand displayed. Even if you had continued playing the machine, you probably would not have won anyway. Your own timing on that next hand would undoubtedly have been different. The royal could be in that 66 to 400 hands that were never displayed. It's like trying to catch a specific raindrop in a downpour. Get the picture?

How To Play

Video poker is like a regular slot machine except that it has a video monitor rather than reels. There is no handle to pull. The typical configuration is an "award glass" above the video screen and a row of buttons below it or beside the screen used to play the game. The configuration may vary with each manufacturer, but the basic game is as described. Variations of the game with wild cards to give you more alternatives may tease or confuse you; we'll describe those later.

Under the coin slot, a deal button is pushed for play after one or more coins are inserted. When the maximum number of coins are inserted, the machine deals automatically. Five cards from a standard 52-card deck appear on the screen. Under each card is a "hold" button so you can choose which cards to keep before pushing the "draw" button to replace the cards not held. Push the "cancel" button to change your hold cards before drawing if you change your mind or accidentally push the wrong hold button. On many machines, there is no "cancel" button: you push the hold button a second time to erase the "hold" and correct a mistake.

BE CAREFUL USING THE *HOLD* BUTTONS. WE HAVE OFTEN SEEN CARELESS PLAYERS HIT THEM SO FAST THAT THEY EITHER DON'T REGISTER OR ELSE THEY REGISTER AS BEING HIT TWICE. EITHER WAY, THE CARD THEY WANT TO HOLD IS ACCIDENTALLY DISCARDED AND MAY RUIN A GREAT HAND OR MISS FILLING IN A POTENTIAL WINNER. *BE SURE ALL CARDS ARE HELD AS YOU INTENDED BEFORE HITTING THE DRAW BUTTON.*

The payout for each winning hand is displayed on the award glass above the screen so that the player may determine in advance what to expect. Some manufacturers now display the payout table on the screen rather than on a separate glass above the screen, so that you can see how the expected return increases with each coin played.

If you have a winner after the draw, the type of hand (two pair, straight, full house, flush, straight flush, etc.) and "winner" are usually displayed on the newer-type screens. As the machine pays by coins or credit, the amount is counted on a meter also displayed on the screen. If the hand is not a winner, "game over" and "insert coin" will be seen, and the machine is ready for the next hand.

Most machines follow this basic playing format. However, some machines also have a "stand" button. If you are dealt a pat hand on the first five cards, remember to push either all hold buttons or the stand button before drawing, or the machine will erase your winning hand. Some machines won't let you lose a good hand; they will pay on a full house, four-of-a-kind, straight flush, and sometimes a full house before you have a chance to draw. Others are not so "kind"; they'll let you throw it away and try to upgrade the hand. Some players actually prefer the choice to the automatic pay. If you hit a royal flush with maximum coins, the jackpot will usually be paid by an attendant.

Other machines have "discard" buttons instead of "hold" buttons. On these machines you push the discard button to throw away unwanted cards.

If you do not discard specific cards, the machine will count your hand as final even if it is a loser.

BE SURE YOU KNOW WHICH TYPE OF MACHINE YOU ARE PLAYING, AND DON'T PUSH THOSE BUTTONS UNTIL YOU UNDERSTAND WHAT YOU ARE DOING.

The Play Buttons

Below or beside the screen are the buttons used to play the game. The number and type vary depending on the manufacturer, the age, or the type of machine being played. Some examples of the most common types are shown below. The original straight draw poker:

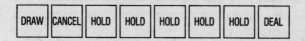

There are still quite a few of these around. On these early machines, the winning coins were dropped when won except for straight and royal flushes which were usually hand paid. Some old-timers still prefer these types and like the jingle of the coins as they hit the tray.

Newer credit types:

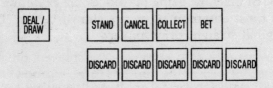

The play button second from left is to play less than the maximum coins. Push once for each coin you wish to play. If you want to play the maximum coins, push the "play max coins" button second from right.

Discard types:

DEAL / DRAW		STAND	CANCEL	COLLECT	BET
		DISCARD	DISCARD	DISCARD	DISCARD	DISCARD

The position and/or label of the different buttons varies with the manufacturer. Our layouts of these buttons are not to scale.

The Video Screen

In the center of the machine at eye level, the TV monitor displays the cards to be played. When you walk up to a vacant machine, you will see either a typical "royal flush" flashing to attract your attention or you will see the last hand that was played on the machine and whether or not it was a winner. It depends on the manufacturer. In the latter case, you will also see the amount of payout, if any, and on the credit machines, the total cash-out of credits by the previous player. Sometimes it may be only a few coins; sometimes it could be several hundred depending upon at which point the player collected his coins and left.

If the last hand played was a royal flush, or a straight flush, or four or five wild cards for a major payout, it was probably hit with less than maximum coins (in which case the machine usually spits out the coins). Most players will play it off before they leave. In fact, casinos will ask you to play off a royal if you have been paid by an attendant.

Sometimes the paytable is displayed on the screen instead of on the award glass above the video screen. If so, you will see the expected payout increase with each coin inserted and the bonus "incentive" if you play the maximum coins required.

The Deal

What most people don't know about these machines is how the cards are dealt from a 52-card deck to prevent the same card from showing up on the "draw" after having been discarded.

When the program "deals" the first five cards on most machines, it also selects five more cards which are placed in a position right behind the ones displayed. Think of it as five stacks of two cards each, both dealt face down when you insert the first coin.

When you push the deal button or play the maximum coins, the top cards in each stack are turned over to show your hand. You play the hand, holding and/or discarding before pushing the draw button. The machine does not deal replacement cards from the top of a stack of five cards or the balance of the deck waiting in the background. Cards are not dealt from left to right in sequence from either stack as would be the case in a table game.

If the first card from the left is discarded (or not held), the card replacing it on the draw will be the card already selected and waiting behind or underneath it, figuratively speaking. If the second card is retained, the card selected and waiting behind it will not be turned over on the draw, and so on. If the card to the extreme right, for instance, is the only one discarded, the card waiting immediately behind it is the one to be displayed, not the first card from an invisible stack of five cards. After the draw, win or lose, the machine deals the next hand from a full deck.

Types Of Machines

The first video poker machines were the 5-card draw poker machines, most with a "6-9" payout table. This shortened description has been adapted by authors and strategists as a means to both identify the "straight" or "regular" version of the game, and, at the same time, distinguish between the two most common variations in payout on that type of machine.

The difference between the "6-9" and the "5-8" types refers to the payout per coin played for flushes and full houses, respectively, on these regular machines (6-9) and the progressive jackpot versions (5-8) of the regular types. **Obviously the "6-9" machine is the one to look for among regular machines since it pays more for a flush and full house.** Complete paytables of these and other types are found in the chapter on percentages.

The appeal of the game to the general public and its rapid rise in popularity beyond that of the "one-armed bandits" can be attributed to several factors:

First, it combines a modicum of skill with the facility of slot playing, made even faster and easier with buttons to push instead of handles to pull.

That modicum of skill is an important facet of video poker's acceptance as a "game," not just a "gamble." It decreases the reliance on chance or luck to win, unlike regular slot machines which have players at the casino's mercy.

Second, it is a "sit down" game with its own attached seat and screen (opponent) at eye level, but without the intimidation that a novice or less-skilled poker player would feel when faced with a live dealer and opponent players at the casino tables.

Third, it is now deemed more "respectable" to participate in a game of "video poker" than to pour money down the hungry gullet of a "plain" slot machine.

Watching the number and face cards being dealt is more fascinating than watching fruits and bells and bars spinning around until they stop (usually on the wrong line.) Making choices on the draw gives a player a sensation of control and power over the outcome; he is not entirely at the machine's mercy.

Like the video arcade games explosion which produced a myriad of imitations and variations, video poker's tremendous success has spurred a revolutionary group of variations that vie for players' attention and purse. Some types were short-lived such as 7-card stud and Red Dog. Both Deuces Wild and Joker Wild types were fairly popular but not numerous until the IGT versions hit the casinos. Let's briefly describe the types that have prevailed and are more popular in some areas than the straight-poker original.

Joker Poker

"Joker poker" or Joker Wild machines were almost an overnight success. The addition of a second best "mini-jackpot" for five-of-a-kind and the increase in size of the royal flush bonus became palatable substitutes for diminished returns on the lesser winning hands. The payout for a "dirty" or "wild" royal with a joker replacing any of the other "royal" members of that group was comparable to that for 4-of-a-kind on a straight machine. Players soon began to line up, so to speak, to play the machines, even to the neglect of the straight types. They were a favorite of locals in Las Vegas and other Nevada casinos and have carried their weight on the casino floor for years.

Deuces Wild

Like Joker Poker, these machines have a "mini" jackpot for four deuces which, on most machines, equals that for 5-of-a-kind on Joker Wild types. They have four wild cards instead of one. Consequently, the smaller winning hands again suffer with a comparable reduction in payout — a sort of "law of diminishing returns."

Players are willing to trade these diminished returns for an "ostensible" increase in possibility of hitting the mini- pot. Think about the flaw in that rationale. It should be easier to get five-of-a-kind (four-of-a-kind of any card in the deck plus the joker) than four of only one card — the deuce.) However, video poker players are fickle. Before long, Deuces Wild machines received more play than Joker Poker and are (what else?) gradually outnumbering those "happy harlequins" in many casinos.

Deuces–Joker Wild

Manufacturers and casinos are always willing to oblige the customers with the games they prefer. Since they enjoyed both one and four wild card poker why not give them five wild cards? Combining the two types and adding yet another jackpot incentive, these machines now have a "maxi-jackpot" for hitting the five wild cards that is 2½ times that of a straight royal flush.

Wow! Who could resist? What's the trade-off? The "mini" jackpots for four deuces, wild royal, and five-of-a-kind diminish proportionately. The return for four-of-a-kind (so nice on 5-8 and 6-9 machines) has dropped from 125 coins to 20 coins, with the same payout for full houses and flushes. A straight flush dropped from 250 to 30 on quarter, half-dollar, and dollar machines. Ugh! Guess what! These machines are becoming popular, but not quite as rapidly as the other two wild machines.

Second Chance

This variation manufactured by Bally is still around, although large banks have become smaller banks, making room for more popular wild types. The machine basically differs from straight poker only by giving the player an opportunity to turn a losing hand into a winner if drawing a sixth card could result in a straight or higher hand (e.g. two pair could become a full house, or three-of-a-kind could become four-of-a-kind or a full house.)

When you are given a ''second chance'' the notice will flash on the screen and/or the 2nd chance button will light up. An odds chart is also displayed with potential payout indicated if it hits. You may then elect to gamble more coins on that draw or decline. If you choose to do so, you push the 2nd chance button and wager from the credit bank (if any) or drop in more coins. With each coin inserted (one through the max), the odds chart will indicate an increase in the payout if you're successful.

Occasionally, the maximum payout will exceed that for the same hand if hit on the first draw.

You need to examine the chart very carefully to determine if the odds and payout are worth the price of that "Second Chance." You may just prefer to start a new game.

Double Up

This game is a modified version of Red Dog. After the deal or draw, you may be given a chance to wager the whole amount won on that hand for "double or nothing." If so, you push the appropriate button and pray. We've seen players become quite "skillful" or lucky at doubling their winnings. Once we saw a player double a royal flush pot on a quarter machine ($2,000 instead of $1,000). We don't know if it was by guts or by accident. That's not playing a game, that's gambling! So much for strategy.

The number and location of these types are minimal compared to the other variations.

Progressives

Progressives are not a separate type of game. We list them here because they have become so prevalent and because of the variations that keep cropping up. As with progressive slots there are two basic types: individual machines with single or multiple jackpots of their own, and banks of machines linked to a single or multiple jackpots.

As the name suggests, the one thing they all have in common is that the jackpot usually starts at a level comparable to the bonus jackpot on an individual straight poker machine of a particular denomination (e.g. $250 for nickels, $1,000 for quarters, $2,000 for half-dollars and $4,000 for dollars). The jackpot increases as machines are played and builds until someone hits the royal flush. It immediately resets at the minimum amount and continues to build until hit again.

These progressives have become the target of team players and "expert strategists" because the jackpots sometimes climb to very attractive figures. We will discuss the calculations and the teams in detail in other sections of the book.

We would be remiss if we failed to mention here that casinos are capitalizing on the widespread interest in progressives by providing more banks of all types. Besides individual and banks of straight poker, we've found progressive banks of:

Joker Poker
Deuces Wild
Deuces-Joker Wild
Combinations of two or all three of the above.

The combination usually displays separate sets of jackpots for each type. Some even have individual progressive pots for other than the royal such as for straight flush, wild cards, all four-of-a-kinds, and even full houses and flushes. There seems to be no end to the ways they try to "reel" in the "catch of the day" to these wild and crazy progressives. Sometimes the small-win jackpots get pretty big, especially if they are fed by unsuspecting or ultra-conservative players who play less than the maximum coins.

The newest progressive is **MegaPoker** developed by EDT to offer a video poker jackpot to compete favorably with the huge slot jackpots. It is a multi-property progressive system. This system is located in bars and restaurants on the EDT route. We have included more information and the math behind MegaPoker in the chapter on Percentages.

Myth-Conceptions

There are dozens of myths and/or misconceptions that have arisen over video poker machines that may mislead players into making wrong decisions about where, when, and how to play. It is time that we debunk some of these "myth-conceptions."

MYTH-CONCEPTION 1:

The machines are controlled by someone in the back room.

Each machine is an independently operating device. Its computer program is set by the manufacturer to a given payback percentage, and the only way to alter it is to physically change the program chips inside the machine.

All of the computer monitoring and player club systems connected to the machines are designed to collect information; they cannot exert any influence on the game.

Even though the technology exists to design such controls, government regulators would not permit such a "master switch" operation. They do not tolerate "cheating" by casinos any more than by players.

MYTH-CONCEPTION 2:

When a mechanic opens a machine, it will stop paying.

There are no switches, knobs, or screws inside a machine that will change how the machine is paying. Most of the time a mechanic or floor-person will open a machine only to clear a coin jam or refill a hopper if you have won enough to empty it. There is no way for the mechanic to "set up" a machine to hit a royal or prevent the machine from selecting a winning hand.

MYTH-CONCEPTION 3:

"I have played this machine for hours — it is due to hit."

It may be "due" or even long "overdue," but that doesn't mean it is "ready" to hit. (As we have said elsewhere, a machine is never "ready" to hit.) Every play is completely independent of every other play. It doesn't matter if you have played a machine for five minutes or five hours; every deal is from a full deck, and the RNG (which selects each hand) has no memory of what has happened before.

The machine's accounting memory which keeps track of the statistical information on the machine performance can recall a specific number of previous hands played (depending on the make and model), but the accounting memory has no effect on subsequent hands selected by the RNG.

MYTH-CONCEPTION 4:

The change-girl can tell you which machine is ready to hit.

Again, every machine and every play is independent. No one in the casino has any "inside information'' on which machines are ready to hit. A change-person or floor-person may tell you if a machine has hit in the last few hours or the day before, if they know. They may also tell you if it has been played a lot without recent success. These factors may help you decide whether or not to play the machine, but neither is any guarantee that it is ready to pay.

MYTH-CONCEPTION 5:
Using a club card makes the machine pay more often.

The player club cards do not affect the operation of the machine. They will not cause the machine to pay more or less often. Some casinos have modified machines to give bonus payouts if you win with a club card in the reader. However, that doesn't increase the frequency of the payouts, just the amount.

MYTH-CONCEPTION 6:
The professional gambler has a better chance than the tourist.

Every player has the same chance of winning. The machine has no way of knowing if you are a tourist or a professional or if you are tall or short. The machine does not care. It has no feelings or bias. The only edge a better player may have is his ability to choose the best cards to hold. Very few people will throw away a flush or a straight, but it does happen. See the chapter on strategies.

MYTH-CONCEPTION 7:

The machine pays better if you use cold coins.

The temperature of the coins doesn't make any difference to the machine. If some coins from the machine are warmer than others, it is only because the inside of the machine is warmer than the outside air. Incandescent instead of fluorescent bulbs in some machines generate heat. The coins get warm in the hopper but soon cool off in the tray. Whether you play coins dropped from the machine or from a fresh roll purchased is immaterial. A coin in the slot only starts the selection process. The RNG does not respond to thermal stimuli in any way.

MYTH-CONCEPTION 8:

The machine you just left was hit by the next player; you should have stuck with it.

The random number generator inside the machine is constantly running and it chooses a new hand every 1000th of a second. Only when you insert a coin or press the deal button is the final hand chosen. For you to have hit that machine, you would have had to hit the deal button at the exact millisecond that the next player did — a very unlikely possibility. The average person has a reaction time of 50 to 350 seconds but the mechanical switch in the machine takes only 16 to 50 milliseconds. That means that 66 to 400 milliseconds is as close as a person could estimate the right time to play, and, in that time, 66 to 400 different hands could be dealt. Maybe next time you'll be the one to hit after someone else has left. The micro-processor controls the time, not you or any other player.

MYTH-CONCEPTION 9:

Playing fast will make the machine pay out more often.

The speed at which you play has no direct effect on whether the machine will pay more often. In fact, if you play too fast, you may hit the deal button before your last coin registers. That could not only cost you a coin but also could cost you more money if you happen to hit a payoff without the maximum coins played. Also, if you draw too fast, you might make the wrong choice or accidentally push a hold button twice and cancel out a winning hand. The buttons are usually very sensitive to the touch, but sometimes one or more may not be as easy to push and may not hold. Playing two-handed for speed can be dangerous even if you're ambidextrous. Sometimes the left hand doesn't know what the right one is doing and vice versa. Don't try to beat the machine at its own speed; you'll lose.

We have seen an old gentleman who frequently plays dollar video poker. He counts, softly but audibly, as fast as he can between plays; and after he inserts his coins, he also presses the deal or draw button as fast as he can. He varies the number of coins he plays, seldom the maximum, but we haven't been able to hear just whether his count is the same or varied. We've never seen him win more than a few coins. He plays only five or six hands before changing machines. His method is fast but futile. He, at best, just spreads his losses around.

MYTH-CONCEPTION 10:

If someone next to you hits a royal, your machine won't hit.

It would be practically impossible to coordinate or synchronize pay cycles on adjacent machines to hit in any specific order. Besides, the random play each machine receives would upset any such ordered responses, not to mention the various strategies used by different players. This myth, at best, is drawing on the "law of averages" and, at worst, superstition. Speaking of superstition, we devoted a whole chapter in *Slot Machine Mania* to describing most of those that players believe in or practice faithfully.

One machine does not know when another machine is dealing or paying. Only on linked progressive machines are the payout meters linked to reset the progressive jackpot after it is hit. This linkage has no effect on the random number generator in each machine that chooses the deal. (i.e. The bank of machines are not controlled by a single RNG; the machines are still individually controlled.) We've seen royals hit side by side within a few seconds or minutes on both individual and progressive machines.

MYTH-CONCEPTION 11:

Everytime they have a drawing, they tighten the machines.

How often we've heard, "I never win during one of these special promotions." Why would a casino deliberately try to keep anyone from winning? A new winner is a new customer who will probably return to play again. If you have bad luck during these drawings, it's probably because someone else was at the right machine at the right time. The casino is happy if all or most of the machines are being played; that is why they hold the drawings — to get more people through the doors.

Changing a machine's percentage involves substituting the computer chips in the machine and revising the award glass. The time involved to change all or most machines on the floor does not justify the effort for short periods of time. Don't worry; their hold percentage is all the casinos need to make their profit.

MYTH-CONCEPTION 12:

The hopper is full, I can hear the coins falling into the bucket below; it must be "ready" to hit.

A full or empty hopper does not mean the machine is ready to pay. It could have been recently refilled by an attendant after running out of coins on a previous payout or cash-out. As you insert coins into the machine, some of them fall into the hopper and some fall into the "drop" bucket under the machine. If the drop bucket has just been exchanged, you hear the loud noise of the coins hitting the bottom of the bucket. Note: the "drop" bucket is not to be confused with the coin tray or well that catches your coins from the machine when you collect for a winning hand.

MYTH-CONCEPTION 13:

"This machine is so slow spitting out the coins, it must be a tight one."

The speed or lack thereof with which the machine pays out on a win has nothing to do with the percentage of payback return or whether, in player's parlance, it is "loose" or "tight." As machines grow old, some parts have to be replaced, such as coin acceptors, and perhaps the casino is just a bit slow in performing the required maintenance.

If the machine is slow-paying, the hopper could also be jammed from a bent coin (sometimes a counterfeit coin, a slug, or a foreign coin) or from being too full. It could also happen simply because the hopper is nearly empty.

If it stops paying, the video screen will flash "call attendant." You will need to push the change button to "light" the candle on top of the machine if it does not automatically flash to alert the change-person or floor-person that there is a problem.

If the machine hits frequently, even if it pays slowly, stick with it until it stops hitting. Again, the only reason to leave a "slow-paying" machine is if it's not hitting winners very often or if you can't tolerate the delay in your play.

MYTH-CONCEPTION 14:

"These video poker machines always deal the card I needed one hand too late."

If you made the wrong choice on the draw, and on the next hand the machine deals you the cards you would like to have had before, don't get upset; they most likely would not have been the ones you would have received if you had drawn differently. As we explained in "Understanding the Machine and the Game," the RNG selects the cards randomly each time from a full deck.

If you have heard other myths or have misconceptions that we haven't described, we hope the information in other chapters will clarify any doubts or reservations you have about the game and your chances of winning.

CHAPTER 3

Poker Percentages

Originally, video poker games were limited to the standard 5-Card Draw with several paytables. However, with manufacturers looking for sales and casinos looking for an edge on their competition, additional varieties of machines were soon to follow. That brought 5-Card Stud, 7-Card Stud, Red Dog, and various other games, each of which had limited popularity. Joker Wild and Deuces Wild machines were the next to be introduced and they have remained popular today.

The latest is a Deuces-Joker Wild with the highest jackpot for five wild cards. These too, are getting lots of play.

As this competition for video poker players becomes more frenzied, casinos offer extra bonuses and special variations — anything to capture your interest or make you think you're getting a better return for your money. Some of the most popular extra bonus types are:

Bonus for 4-of-a-kind:
(e.g. 4 aces — highest bonus;
Four 2's, 3's or 4's — next highest bonus;
Four 5's through kings — lowest bonus;
or other combinations purely at the casino's whim.)

Bonus for a Royal Flush of a Specific Suit:
Some of these can be quite large. (e.g.
$2,500 for Hearts on a quarter machine
or $5,000 for Spades on a half-dollar
machine)

Bonus for an Ordered Royal Flush:
(usually A K Q J 10 but can be in reverse
only (10 J Q K A) or either direction —
depends upon the casinos' posted rules)

Bonus for an Ordered Royal Flush in a specific suit:

(Again, the casino decides which of the four suits and what order is the designated bonus winner.)

Bonus for your Favorite 4-of-a-Kind:

(e.g. If 3 is your lucky number or you have a favorite face card — you program the machine to pay on that card. If it hits all four, you win the bonus.)

These bonus hands are just a way of confusing the basic paytables. They are "flagged" in different ways to attract the player, usually highlighted in a different color on the award glass and/or on the "logo" glass below the buttons. The amount of the bonus varies from casino to casino, according to the whim or "generosity" of the particular house.

Some casinos have Bonus Deuces Wild with double the jackpot ($500) for the four wild cards as the second best payout on a quarter machine. The win for a royal flush with wild cards and for a straight flush are considerably reduced.

Other places offer a bonus of only $100 for four deuces. In the long run, you'll pay for the bonus. On these bonus machines the casino's hold percentage is usually assured by reducing the payout for smaller wins on other hands. For example, they may eliminate coins paid for Jacks-or-Better and/or two pair.

The casino hopes that if a player scores on an extra bonus type (or any other type for that matter), he's likely to get "hooked" on that type and play it exclusively for several sessions trying to repeat his good fortune. Additionally, **all of these variations allow the casino to use machines which have lower payback percentages without upsetting the player, because the bonuses make the percentages harder to determine.** One thing has not changed however. You can still look at a video poker paytable and calculate exactly what the payback percentage is.

Tables and Calculations

The following tables show the payback percentages of the most common video poker machines. These are the generally accepted percentages throughout the gaming industry:

Standard Poker Paytables

	5-6	5-7	5-8	6-9
ROYAL FLUSH	250/4,000	250/4,000	250/4,000	250/4,000
STRAIGHT FLUSH	50	50	50	50
FOUR-OF-A-KIND	25	25	25	25
FULL HOUSE	6	7	8	9
FLUSH	5	5	5	6
STRAIGHT	4	4	4	4
THREE-OF-A-KIND	3	3	3	3
TWO PAIR	2	2	2	2
JACKS-OR-BETTER	1	1	1	1
EXPECTED RETURN	91.3-93.4	92.5-94.6	93.7-95.7	95.7-97.7
OPTIMUM PLAY	95.4	96.6	97.7	99.7

The headings on this chart identify the different types of machines by the payout for a flush and full house respectively, such as "6–9," meaning that six coins are paid out (per coin played) for a flush, and nine coins are paid out (per coin played) for a full house.

Always check the paytable on the feature glass (or on the screen) of the machines you wish to play. Find the machine with the best payback percentages.

Wild Card Paytables

	DEUCES WILD	JOKER WILD	DEUCE/JOKER	BONUS DEUCES
5 WILDS	—	—	1000/10,000	—
ROYAL FLUSH NO WILD	250/4000	400/4700	250/4000	250/4000
4 DEUCES NO JOKER	200	—	25	200/2000
ROYAL FLUSH W/WILD	25	100	12	20
5-OF-A-KIND	15	200	9	10
STRAIGHT FLUSH	9	50	6	10
4-OF-A-KIND	5	15	3	4
FULL HOUSE	3	7	3	4
FLUSH	2	5	3	3
STRAIGHT	2	3	2	2
3-OF-A-KIND	1	2	1	1
2 PAIR	—	1	—	—
KINGS-OR-BETTER	—	1	—	—
EXPECTED RETURN	95.3–97.3	92.6–94.6	93.6–95.6	91.6–93.6
OPTIMUM RETURN	99.3	96.6	97.6	95.6

You will notice that these tables indicate the expected return for each paytable. It is the value that the casino expects, and it is what *you* should expect. Depending upon how you play, your returns should fall somewhere within this range over the long haul. Anything can happen in short-term play, but the more you play, the closer the average payback percentage gets to the expected return.

These tables also indicate the optimum percentage, which is the mathematical estimate of the machine's payback if you choose the absolutely correct draw for every hand. **In nearly 20 years in the gaming industry, I have never seen a poker machine return its optimum percentage.**

Suprisingly, I have had dozens of slot managers tell me that they are getting *optimum* play on their machines; however, every time we look at their results, the numbers fall either within the *expected* range, or below. As slot managers become more educated about percentages, and look at them over the long term, they are realizing (and telling us) that the machines are giving them the expected values, *and more.* Today, the slot managers are *not* complaining. It's going to take a lot of education *on the part of the players* to drive the percentages into the upper realm of the expected values. Only a few truly educated players will be able to achieve *optimum* play.

One thing is sure: The gaming industry has accepted these values as correct if for no other reason than *that is how the machines perform.* What better reason could they have? They take it to the bank.

The following tables show how the return for a 5-8 paytable is calculated by a major manufacturer, and a major casino. The third chart shows actual meter values taken from 15 machines in a very popular location. These charts are rarely, if ever, seen by the gaming public.

Pay Table Calculation From a Major Manufacturer*

Jacks-or-Better (Hit Freq 45.82%)

	Odds to 1	Hit Frequency %	Pays	Payback %
Jacks-or-Better	4.58	21.8200	1	21.8200
2 Pair	7.76	12.8800	2	25.7600
3-of-a-Kind	13.39	7.4700	3	22.4100
Straight	84.75	1.1800	4	4.7200
Flush	93.46	1.0700	5	5.3500
Full House	86.96	1.1500	8	9.2000
4-of-a-Kind	416.67	0.2400	25	6.0000
Straight Flush	10,000.00	0.0100	50	0.5000
Royal Flush	40,000.00	0.0025	250	0.6250
		0.0025	800**	2.0000
		45.8225		96.3850 1–4 COIN
				97.7600 5 COIN

*Based on theoretical results.

**Since this chart is based on 1 coin played, the computation for a 5-coin royal (4,000-coin payoff) is 800 coins (4,000 ÷ 5).

Pay Table Calculation From a Major Casino*

	Odds to 1	Hit Frequency %	Number of Hits	Each Paid	Total Coins Out	Payback %
Jacks-or-Better	5.00	20.0000	9238	1	9238	20.0000
2 Pair	8.00	12.4984	5773	2	11546	24.9967
3-of-a-Kind	14.00	7.1422	3299	3	9897	21.4267
Straight	87.15	1.1474	530	4	2120	4.5897
Flush	90.04	1.1106	513	5	2565	5.5535
Full House	89.17	1.1215	518	8	4144	8.9716
4-of-a-Kind	444.13	0.2252	104	25	2600	5.6289
Straight Flush	11,547.50	0.0087	4	50	200	0.4329
Royal Flush	46,190.00	0.0022	1	800**	4000	1.7319
		43.2540	19,980		43110	93.3319

Total coins in: 46,190

*Based on actual results.

**Since this chart is based on 1 coin played, the computation for a 5-coin royal (4,000-coin payoff) is 800 coins (4,000 ÷ 5).

Actual Meter Readings

Coins	In 61,951,644				Out 58,282,630		Out w/ Jackpots 59,296,184	
	Hits Per Coins Played						Hit	Odds
	1	2	3	4	5	Total	Frequency %	to 1
Royal	60	59	34	6	249	408	0.002420	41,325.45
SF	239	235	118	17	911	1,520	0.009015	11,092.62
4K	6,007	6,764	3,031	603	22,657	39,062	0.231674	431.64
Full	30,068	32,869	14,482	2,914	109,216	189,549	1.124200	88.95
Flush	29,276	31,393	14,223	2,962	105,809	183,663	1.089291	91.80
St	29,974	32,544	14,196	2,856	105,019	184,589	1.094783	91.34
3K	195,584	214,700	94,362	19,552	715,058	1,239,256	7.349931	13.61
2 Pair	339,670	372,305	164,915	33,276	1,242,290	2,152,456	12.766049	7.83
Jacks	574,234	623,734	274,491	55,943	2,056,050	3,584,452	21.259105	4.70
	1,205,112	1,314,603	579,852	118,129	4,357,259	7,574,955	44.93	Payback %
								95.71
Games	2,682,410	2,926,121	1,290,669	262,938	9,698,646	16,860,784		

The first thing you should have noticed from these charts is that the actual payback percentage of a machine evaluated in real casino play was considerably less than the calculation from a major manufacturer. Compare the theoretical hold percentge of 97.7600 to the real-world results of 93.3319. It's a glaring discrepancy that supports our position that these machines are holding more than they are supposed to. In fact, the casinos are profiting more than the machines have been programmed to give them!

Players are simply making mistakes in strategy, or using the wrong strategy, or not using any strategy at all! Casinos are making all kinds of money. Let's not make it any easier for them!

The second thing worth noting is the wide variations in these charts beyond the hold percentages. Beyond what we've just discussed, another reason for these vatiations, even in theory, is that no one can agree on how often a given type of hand will actually occur.

People play the machines differently. And even in strict theory, there is disagreement. The royal flush is the one that is the most controversial. If you throw away everything (including winning hands like four-of-a-kind) and only play for the royal flush, you should average one every 21,000 hands. If you play a more profitable strategy by not throwing away winners, you should see the royal flush less often. But how much less often? That is where everyone seems to disagree. Most of the strategies are very similar, but their numbers are slightly different. Let's see if we can clarify the matter.

You can expect to be dealt a royal once in every 650,000 hands. You can expect to be dealt four cards to the royal and draw to it once in every 130,000 hands, and you can expect to be dealt three cards to the royal and draw to it once in every 65,000 hands.

If you added these three associated probabilities you would expect to get a royal flush about every 40,000 hands. That assumes that you have not kept any other winners and that you didn't draw 3, 4, or 5 cards to a royal at any time. Most people in the industry seem to like and accept the estimate of 40,000 hands.

In the Strategy chapter, we explain the flaws in the strategies being proposed by the experts in their video poker books. That chapter is by far the most important of our book, and is what sets our book apart from all the others.

Progressive Calculations

Progressive machines are those that have a bonus payout for certain hands that increases as the machine is played. Typically, a group of machines are connected to a sign that displays the dollar amount you would receive for hitting a royal flush with the maximum coins played. You can watch the metered display adding each penny or fraction thereof to the jackpot as the coins are inserted. To determine the payback percentage of a progressive machine you take the base percentage of the machine and add the amount of the progressive increment.

For Example:

Standard Quarter Draw Poker Machines with 5-8 Paytable
Normal payback percentage = 95.3
Progressive Reset Value 4000 coins = $1000
Increment Percentage = 0.5% of Coin-In (Increment of 5 coins for every 1000 played — $1.25 for every $250 played)
Expected Payback Percentage = 95.3 + 0.5 = 95.8

As you can see, most progressive jackpots increase at the rate of one-half of one percent of all coins played, (e.g. .005 or 5 cents for every $10.00 played.)

Collecting The "Drop"

On the larger progressives, the casino actually takes the progressive increment out of the machine's drop and puts the money into a special interest-bearing account from which they pay the jackpot. (The machine's "drop" is the actual coins that fall into the bucket inside the stand below the machine.)

The drop is collected periodically, usually daily, and taken to the counting room where the coins are counted and re-rolled to be resold to the players. If you should happen to play during the "wee" hours of the morning you'll see the carts loaded with buckets of money collected. You will be asked to step aside from your machine while the buckets are exchanged. After the exchange, you can actually hear some of the coins you play dropping into the empty bucket below. As the bucket fills, the sound becomes muffled and inaudible in the noisy casino.

In the counting room, the drop is compared to the computer printout of the meter readings on the machine. The printout usually shows the coin-in/coin-out totals (i.e. coins played and coins paid out by the machine.) Royal flushes and other hand-pay amounts are also registered.

When a machine's payout hopper is empty, it is refilled by a casino attendant and recorded on a form. Refills are usually witnessed by two or more employees and entered into the accounting records.

These records are important to determine which machines are holding to their programmed per-

centage and making money for the casino. You
can bet that if they don't, they will be examined
carefully to find out why not and either repaired
or yanked from the floor and replaced with new
"reliables."

For instance, the casinos use the following for-
mulas to determine the machine's performance:

WIN = Drop – (Fills + Hand-Paid Jackpots)
WIN = Coins In x Theoretical Hold Percentage
WIN/COIN IN = ACTUAL HOLD PER-
CENTAGE

For those machines that do not start the
progressive at the normal non-progressive payout
for the royal flush (4,000 coins), you will have to
calculate what the additional progressive amount
represents and add it to the calculation. For example, a jackpot starts at $10,000 and progresses at
two-tenths of one percent. Assuming it is expected
to hit around $15,000, the .002 increment factor
represents $5,000 of the progressive and the
$10,000 represents another four-tenths of one per-
cent. Therefore, the total payback of the machine
would be the original payback percentage plus six-
tenths of one percent (.006).

Progressive Teams

As casinos compete for their share of video poker players, they link more and more machines into progressive jackpots. The more players trying for a single jackpot, the quicker it climbs, sometimes to very attractive figures. Attractive enough for gambling entrepreneurs to form teams to tie down all the machines in a bank or at least as many as possible. Players are recruited to "work" for an hourly rate playing the machines. These "professionals" study the math on odds and probabilities and try to estimate the approximate cost of hitting the jackpot. They scout the progressive jackpots, and when they find one high enough to exceed their cost estimate, they "send in the clowns to go for broke." They sometimes *do* go broke trying to "break the bank."

How do the casinos feel about the "professional" teams? They tolerate them as long as other players don't complain. After all, casinos want the best action they can get for around-the-clock revenue. In fact, one casino in Northern Nevada used to "comp" team players with food and lodging during the winter months when business was slow. The bottom-line revenue looked fine with the play level relatively consistent. However, in the long run it proved to be detrimental. The teams walked out the door with the big jackpots.

Tourists and locals who were unable to get a seat at a bank with a large progressive became disenchanted with that particular casino and took their playing money elsewhere.

Many players traditionally return to the place where they've won and eventually play back their winnings.

Casinos have learned that hundreds or thousands of steady customers are more important for the bottom line than a few teams of a few dozen players who "hit and split." As one casino manager once said, "I would rather give out a hundred $1,000 jackpots instead of one $100,000 jackpot."

We interviewed a former progressive "team chief." Claude (not his real name) operated teams in the early days of video poker, primarily in Northern Nevada where the progressive pots were high enough to justify the risk. Las Vegas and Atlantic City progressives seldom reached the estimated profit-peaks. Claude paid his quarter players $6.00 per hour and dollar players $10.00 per hour. Not a bad wage for playing a simple game of poker. Everyone would like to get rich "playing" their favorite game, even when it turns into "work."

On one occasion, Claude put his team on a bank of six quarter machines with a jackpot of $4,000 and hit within 15 minutes for a net profit of almost the whole four grand. That's the *good* news!

On another occasion, Claude's team tried for a $13,000 pot on a bank of twelve dollar machines. After he spent $27,000, it finally hit for a net loss of $14,000. That's the *bad* news! It took a lot more plays to hit the Royal than he anticipated. It isn't hard to imagine the terrible feeling he had as his losses and expenses exceeded the amount of the jackpot. They couldn't stop; they had to chase the progressive to try to recoup some of the money. IN GAMBLING, NOTHING IS CERTAIN BUT UNCERTAINTY.

The main factor to consider in estimating the cost of winning a jackpot is the basic cost for playing the probable number of hands to win. Assuming an expert player uses an Optimum strategy consistently on a 95 percent payback quarter machine, he should expect to hit the royal in approximately 40,000 hands. At five coins per hand, the basic formula is 40,000 x $1.25 = $50,000 minus the expected return of 95% of that amount or $47,500. That computes to $2,500, a substantial bankroll for starters. The target jackpot for an individual player must exceed $2,500 to be worth the investment. For a dollar machine, the target jackpot would be $5.00 x 40,000 = $200,000 - $190,000 = $10,000.

In addition to the basic cost computed above, progressive teams must add the wages for team players to calculate the size of the target jackpot. Time translates into money. If one player averages 320 hands per hour, it would take him 125 hours to score.

Stanford Wong's book, *Professional Video Poker Strategy,* outlined a strategy for progressives and calculated the size of jackpots needed to overcome the expected value. His examples included 5-8 quarter progressive machines requiring jackpots as high as $5,000 to $10,000 to reach certain break-even points. Quarter jackpots that high for video poker are now very rare and probably non-existent. Further, Wong states that you can play 500 hands per hour and a "professional" player could hit 700. That's practically impossible. It would take another machine (a pretty smart robot) to play the machine that fast.

Even on the credit machines, six hands a minute (360 an hour) is extremely fast. In fact, 320 hands is the typical number used by teams that used to operate in Northern Nevada. How do they figure that amount? They have to take into account all the human factors that interfere with constant rapid play as well as the machine payouts.

For instance, ten seconds to deal, select and draw may be adequate for a seasoned veteran with excellent reflexes and manual dexterity to feed the coins into the slot and push two to seven buttons — all the while maintaining a steady rhythm. However, that ten seconds must also allow time for the machine to spit out coins or chalk up credits for the small wins. We doubt that any efficiency expert would disagree. Further, no single player could survive a 125-hour marathon without food, sleep, nature calls and a shower or two. Don't forget the interruptions for comp drinks, to scratch your nose, to puff a cigarette, to buy more coins, or to wait for a floorman to correct an occasional machine malfunction. As you can see, 320 hands per hour is more realistic than 360.

Progressive teams would have to change shifts on each machine to tie it up around the clock. Assuming one of the machines in a bank finally hits in the estimated 125 hours, the team cost per player-hour could be $6.00 x 125 = $750 for a quarter machine and $10.00 x 125 = $1,250 for a dollar jackpot. If the team ties up all 12 machines, and if Lady Luck feels generous and gives them a royal within the first hour, the team cost in wages alone for that one hour would be 12 x $6.00 = $72 for the quarter and $120 for the dollar machines. That cost escalates with each hour it takes to win.

Claude told us of several other hazards he encountered managing progressive teams. As an incentive to speed up the team play, he offered bonuses. Before long, the payback percentage dropped from 95% to 90%. He caught players discarding winning hands so the machine would not slow them down — by making them push extra buttons or wait for coins paid out or credits tabulated — just so they could get the bonus.

Another time Claude discovered some team members making side bets on who would get the highest hand in the next hour. He caught players discarding a one-card draw to a Royal Flush (a 1 in 47 shot) to hold a pair of high cards for a better chance at a full house or four-of-a-kind. No wonder Claude is a "former" team chief.

Actually, the reason Claude is no longer running progressive teams is that the IRS wanted him to withhold income and social security taxes on his employees, the players. Apparently, the profits from running teams didn't justify running a full-time "business" subject to all the headaches of licensing, bookkeeping, audits, taxes, etc. Can't you just picture the advertisement for team players?

> WANTED: Video poker players. Share in big jackpots or "work" for an hourly rate. Speed training will be provided. Must be honorable and healthy. Non-smokers preferred. No chain smokers or gossips. Those suffering from weak

eyes, weak bladders, arthritis, allergies,
or sticky fingers need not apply.

Claude's experience reminds us of the story
John Gollehon, our publisher, told us of a fel-
low who used to "book" his friends' keno wagers.
When they won, he would pay them; when they
lost, he pocketed their money. He was confident
of never having to pay the big jackpot because
the odds on Keno are one of the worst of any game
in the casino. Apparently, he did quite well as a
"Keno bookie."

The following table shows a typical calculation
for a progressive team. A quick look shows that
the cost for a 5-8 quarter machine is $3,250. The
progressive would have to be at least that high for
you to break even, let alone make a profit. The
value listed as "dollars lost" is your break-even
point. However, spending five days of your life
trying for a jackpot that only lets you break even
is hardly worth the effort or the investment. It
wouldn't even be fun.

Progressive Team Calculations

Paytable	5–8 Quarter	6–9 Dollar
Machine Percentage	$0.95	$0.97
Dollars per Play	$1.25	$5.00
Estimated Plays Needed To Hit Royal Flush	40,000.00	40,000.00
Dollars Played into Machine	$50,000.00	$200,000.00
Dollars Payback from machine	$47,500.00	$194,000.00
Expected Dollars Lost	$2,500.00	$6,000.00
Plays per Hour	$320.00	$320.00
Loss per Hour	$20.00	$48.00
Estimated Hours to Hit Royal Flush	125.00	125.00
Pay Rate for Players	$6.00	$10.00
Payroll Till Hit	$750.00	$1,250.00
Total Cost to Hit Jackpot	$3,250.00	$7,250.00
Add 20% for variance	$650.00	$1,450.00
Break-even Jackpot Amount	$3,900.00	$8,700.00

If you're considering recruiting or joining a progressive team, think again. Instead, focus your sights on the type of machine that is most entertaining for you and offers the best paytable to fit the strategy you prefer. Keep play sessions from turning into frustrating marathons to win at all costs.

MegaPoker

In order to offer a video poker jackpot high enough to compare favorably with the huge slot jackpots, Electronic Data Technologies (EDT) has created a multi-property progressive system for poker. The gaming industry refers to these multi-property types as "wide-area progressives." The EDT MegaPoker system is essentially the same as the IGT MegaBucks, a state-wide slot machine progressive, except that it is designed for video poker machines instead of slots. Since EDT is one of the largest route operators in Nevada, it is understandable that you will find these machines in the bars and restaurants on the EDT route.* At this writing they can be found in locations throughout the state. The MegaPoker machine is

---

*Slot machine routes cover those locations such as bars, restaurants, supermarkets, etc., which have a limited number of machines owned and serviced by route operators, much the same as other vending machine routes. The establishment normally receives a percentage of the profits from the operation.

a standard, 5-coin, 5-8 video poker game with an added progressive payout for an ordered royal flush (A K Q J 10). The quarter progressive starts at $20,000 and grows at a rate of about two cents for every $10.00 played. It is estimated that the progressive should hit about once a month with a value around $30,000 paid all at one time — unlike some large slot progressive pots which are paid incrementally over a specific number of years.

Even though the math related to a jackpot is correct and all of the information looks good, the real world, fate, or human folly has a way of making results somewhat unpredictable. When EDT started the MegaPoker system, the jackpot was hit for $29,313, which was about what was expected. However, the next hit was not so simple. The jackpot continued to grow to over $90,000 before being hit. EDT was even getting complaints that the jackpot never hit. In reality, the ordered royal flush was hit at least five times by "uninformed" players who did not insert the maximum five coins. Therefore, in order to counter the "mis-perception" that MegaPoker never hits, EDT put out placards like "wanted posters" showing the hits with less than maximum coins played. We call it their "Hall of Shame."

Can you imagine how dejected those players must have felt, knowing that they were a quarter or two away from changing their lives? At least $20,000 to $70,000 would change our lives. In fact, one bartender didn't even tell the player that she had blown it. He was probably afraid that she would "kill the messenger" or worse, stop playing. REMEMBER, ALWAYS PLAY THE MAXIMUM COINS.

MegaPoker Math

An ordered royal flush like the one required to win the MegaPoker jackpot should occur once in every 120 regular royal flushes, which is about once in every 4,800,000 hands. If you discarded everything and went for the ordered royal every hand, you could reduce the odds to one in 2,537,625. However, you would have to throw away 4-of-a-kinds and full houses to reach those odds, *which is NOT recommended.* The only time you would have a reason to change the way you play would be when the jackpot exceeded $60,000, and then it would only mean keeping the Ace and Ten of the same suit if they were dealt in the correct positions and discarding the three middle cards.

These wide-area progressives are becoming quite popular. IGT created MegaBucks, Quatermania, and Nevada Nickels. EDT has Quarter

MegaPoker. Can Dollar MegaPoker be far behind?

When EDT bought some assets from Imagineering, they also acquired the name "MegaKeno." What else could be in the works? MegaBingo? MegaDice? The possibilities exist, but we will leave this "Mega-Mania" for another book.

CHAPTER 4

Strategies

If video poker is a game of skill, then there should be a way of developing that skill. Right? Well — maybe. The only skill involved is in learning what cards to keep and what cards to throw away. It's called your "playing strategy."

Anyone who plays frequently will soon develop a pattern of play that he uses most of the time. Unfortunately, the strategies that work in a table game of draw poker don't always work with video poker. Consequently, authors and purported "experts" want to sell you their books describing their "sure-fire" strategies.

There are theoretical experts at mathematics, experts at probabilities and statistics, experts at building tables, even experts at writing about applying all these to playing video poker; but there are few "expert" video poker players.

As with the blackjack card-counting and strategy books of the past, these authors may make more money selling their books than they ever could playing video poker. So beware.

The best anyone can hope for is developing a degree of skill at choosing the cards on the draw that will most likely upgrade a hand to a win or occasionally to a higher winner.

Calculating your Chances

There are several ways used to determine the best cards to draw for a given hand. The first is to look at the probability of drawing the various winning hands possible and after the initial deal to go for the one with the highest probability of being drawn. It would be the best choice if all winning hands had equal payouts, but they don't. The payout varies according to the ranking of the hands. With each different payout, another variable enters the mathematical equation and increases the number of choices.

The second method takes the probability of each draw and multiplies it by the payout for each hand. This method gives you the **expected value** for each draw. You would then choose the hand with the highest expected value which is the method used by most of the experts writing video poker books. Let's look at a simple example of this calculation for a "hypothetical machine" that pays out for each roll of one die.

Roll of One Die

Die	Probability	Payout	Expected Value
1	.166	1	.166
2	.166	1	.166
3	.166	2	.333
4	.166	3	.499
5	.166	1	.166
6	.166	1	.166

Assuming the payouts as shown, you can see that if you were playing such a machine, you would always bet on the "4" because it has the highest expected value, i.e. .166 x 3 = .499.

More often than not, the strategies offered for large progressive jackpots slant the expected values toward the royal flush at the expense of smaller jackpots.

The important thing to remember is that anything can happen during the short term. The

machine does, in fact, have streaks of payouts and droughts. These streaks can last a few hands or many hands; it is not possible to know how long they will last. They also vary from machine to machine, and are not even consistent on a single machine. If they were, the results would become predictable, and the casino would lose its edge.

Incidentally, some machines are labeled as "Player's Edge." That only means you'll be sitting on the "edge of your seat" anticipating a royal. Actually, it's just another name for a different model.

The Flaw in the Strategies

Of the several strategy books and/or computer programs that authors have written on how to play video poker, most (not all) appear to be mathematically correct. However, they all have forgotten the most important factor — "The Real World."

When you work with probability and statistics, you use terms like "sample space," "a statistically significant sample," "standard deviation," "expected value," and "variance." These terms are all well and good, but they don't mean anything to the average player.

In fact, the procedures to analyze statistics are quite complex, and require the services of a true statistician. It is possible that in the case of video poker, all the right statistics have not been properly addressed.

Let's take a simple example like flipping a coin. You have two possible outcomes, heads or tails, (assuming it's a fair coin). So this event has a cycle of two, i.e. two possible results. Each result has an equal probability.

Formula:
$$\frac{1 \text{ occurrence}}{2 \text{ possible}} = .5 \text{ probability}$$
(i.e. each has a 50% chance of occurring)

Therefore, you would expect that if you flipped the coin twice you would get a head once and a tail once. However, you could get a head both times or a tail both times. Everybody knows that the more times you flip the coin, the closer the number of heads and tails will come *as a percentage* to being equal. But the actual number of results will likely fall farther and farther away from the norm. In the case of real dollars wagered, the longer you play, even in a fair game, the percentages may approach the norm, but the actual dollars won or lost will grow larger and larger, and farther away from the true break-even point. It's difficult for many players to comprehend, but then again, it's difficult to comprehend the laws of large numbers, even for an expert.

If you flip the coin 10 times and get 7 heads and 3 tails it still doesn't change the odds: it just means that the number of trials is insufficient to average out yet.

So how many trials is enough? In the field of statistics, it is generally accepted that you need 10 to 50 cycles of the event to have enough trials. For something as simple as flipping a coin, the odds are simple enough that 10 to 20 cycles or 20 to 40 flips should be enough for results to average out. But do you really think it would every time you try? Of course not.

Calculating the probabilities for video poker is far from being so simple. If there were only two different cards in the game, one winner and one loser, the 50 - 50 chance and probabilities of drawing a winner each time might average out at the end of 20 to 40 draws. With each variable introduced, i.e. increased number of cards plus increased number of different payouts, the exponential possibilities and probabilities become almost galactic. It's like reaching for a single star in the milky way. Let's continue your voyage to that almost "unreachable star."

Everyone calculates *their* strategy based upon a machine cycle of 2,598,960 — the number of different 5-card hands you can be dealt initially — and they simply apply their strategy to determine the best draw. Theoretically, if you play the

2,598,960 hands, you should see every possible combination, and your winnings should average out to the payback percentage claimed. However, as we just learned from flipping a coin, in practice you will not always see every possible occurrence in the 2,598,960 hands. So for the strategies to "statistically" average out, you will have to play at least 10 cycles of the machine or 25,989,600 hands. Since video poker is considerably more complicated than flipping a coin, you will probably have to play closer to 50 cycles or 1,299,480,000 hands to obtain the expected average. That's almost 1.3 billion hands, a very long run indeed! Have you experienced "weightlessness" yet?

To put it another way, if you played a game every 10 seconds for every minute of every hour for 24 hours a day, every day, you would reach one cycle of the machine in 300 + days. It hardly seems worth it. If you want to wait for ten cycles, can you sit still for 8 + years? In fact, **most people do not have the time or the inclination to sit through the relatively fewer 40,000 hands needed, on average, to hit a royal flush.** In fact, if you play 40,000 hands, you only have a 65 percent chance of hitting it. You would have to play about 100,000 hands to have a 91 percent chance of hitting a royal flush. Ah! That's the "star" you're reaching for!

The average player will only play several thousand hands during a single session or group of sessions on a few days' trip. For example, a six-to eight-hour visit would enable you to play 1,800 to 2,400 hands. That is less than 20 percent of the estimated games needed to hit a straight flush — let alone a royal. On a typical gambling trip, the number of hands you will play is not enough for you to realistically expect to hit the "Big One." (And we don't mean an earthquake!) Statistically speaking, this sample is too small to be significant. You'll have to rely on "luck" which is literally sitting down to the right machine at the right time — when it *happens* to hit. Contrary to the usual term in player's parlance, a machine is never *ready* to hit. Oops! That star just zipped by!

Additionally, all of these strategies are based upon the probabilities of the game, not the way you play. For example, the math does not take into account the fact that you do not start with $1,250, play 1,000 hands and then count your winnings. The fact is you start with a small stake like $50. You play that and then you play back your winnings, usually until you either hit a big jackpot or lose your stake. *You must have a sufficient stake in order to survive the dry spells; otherwise you won't be around for the long haul.*

The real payback of the machine varies greatly during any short term of play. On the following page, the top chart shows a graph of the type of paybacks you could actually see during a short-term session of play. It is not even close to a single "cycle."

The problem is that this chart could represent five minutes of play or five hours of play. The game is that unpredictable. The chart shows lots of peaks and valleys; these are the winning and losing streaks that the machine goes through while you are playing it.

Again, the winning and losing "streaks" could last five minutes, five hours, or five *days*; and they would not even be consistent in length either way. If you don't have a stake big enough to ride out the losing streaks, you could be going home very early. Thump! You're back to the real world!

The bottom chart shows how the payback percentage averages out for the casino over several months.

Remember, the players play for hours, even days. But the casino is *always* playing. That's why their chart looks a little smoother than the players. It's another example of short-term vs. long-term expectations.

All the casino wants is a small edge, and a long term to make it work for them.

Where most players don't have the stake or the time to ride out severe losing streaks, the casinos have both bases covered. They certainly have the money, and they have all the time in the world.

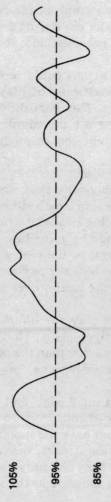

**Example of Players Short-Term Payback Trend.
This could be 5 minutes or 5 days.**

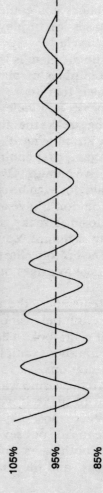

**Example of Casino's Long-Term Payback.
This interval is over millions of hands.**

Three Strategies

Most strategists base their calculations on long-term play to get the best "average" possible. We offer three different short-term strategies for you to consider in playing straight video poker.

We offer this unique concept in strategies, because, as we said before, almost all players play in the short term.

The first is **THE OPTIMUM STRATEGY**. It is designed to be the most consistent for the frequent player who is not playing long enough per session to seriously chase the big jackpots. The profitability for a given session will vary greatly, but it should average out over time to the upper limits of the expected return for the machine.

The second is **THE ROYAL STRATEGY**. It is designed for those players who want to chase the big progressive jackpots without skewing their draws too much toward the large progressive. The Royal Strategy should return a little less over a short run than the Optimum Strategy unless you hit the progressive soon enough to make it profitable. And that's the key to making it work for you. It's a short-term strategy — with a great deal of risk — to maximize your chances of hitting the royal.

The third is **THE CONSERVATIVE STRAT-EGY.** It is designed for the short-term player, also, who is looking for entertainment only and wants to play as long as possible on a limited budget. It, too, should return a little less than the Optimum over the long haul, but can help you in short-term play by increasing your "staying power" at the machines.

All strategists offer tables to memorize or carry along to consult while playing. On the pages that follow, we've included a table for each of the three described above. Feel free to copy and take them along for reference while you play.

The following is a list of the incredibly obvious "pat" hands that have not been included in our tables. The payout for each is high enough to keep the hand. We will discuss a couple of possible "exceptions" later.

Hand Dealt	Draw
Royal Flush	Stand
Straight Flush	Stand
Four-of-a-Kind	Stand
Full House	Stand
Flush	Stand
Straight	Stand

Optimum Strategy

High Cards = Ace, King, Queen, Jack
Gap = two non-consecutive cards, e.g. a 6 and an 8

Hand Dealt	Number to Draw
Four Cards to a Royal	1
Three-of-a-Kind	2
Four Card Straight Flush	1
Two Pair	1
Three Cards to a Royal	2
High Pair	3
Four Card Flush	1
Open End Straight w/3 high cards	1
Low Pair	3
Open End Straight	1
Three to a Straight Flush	2
Two to a Royal – no 10	3
Inside Straight – 3+ high cards	1
Two to a Royal with 10	3
Three High Cards	2
Three to a Straight Flush w/gap	2
Two High Cards	3
One High Card	4
Mixed low cards	5

Start at the top and work down until you find the first draw that fits your hand and use it.

Royal Strategy

High Cards = Ace, King, Queen, Jack
Gap = two non-consecutive cards e.g. a 6 and an 8

Hand Dealt	Number to Draw
Four Cards to a Royal	1
Three-of-a-Kind	2
Four Card Straight Flush	1
Three Cards to a Royal	2
Two Pair	1
High Pair	3
Four Card Flush	1
Open End Straight	1
Low Pair	3
Two to a Royal	3
Three to a Straight Flush	2
Inside Straight – 3+ high cards	1
Three to a Straight Flush w/gap	2
Three High Cards	2
Two High Cards	3
One High Card	4
Mixed low cards	5

Start at the top and work down until you find the first draw that fits your hand and use it.

As an exception to the pat hands mentioned earlier, it should be noted that, depending on the jackpot, the Royal Strategy player would not keep a straight as a pat hand if four of those cards are of the same suit:

10◇ J◇ Q◇ A◇ K♡
Discard the K♡ and try for the K◇.
9♡ 10♣ J♣ Q♣ K♣
Keep face cards (suited) and discard 9♡, looking for the A♣.

Conservative Strategy

High Cards = Ace, King, Queen, Jack
Gap = two non-consecutive cards e.g. a 6 and an 8

Hand Dealt	Number to Draw
Four Cards to a Royal	1
Three-of-a-Kind	2
Four Card Straight Flush	1
Two Pair	1
High Pair	3
Three Cards to a Royal	2
Four Card Flush	1
Low Pair	3
Open End Straight	1
Three to a Straight Flush	2
Two to a Royal	3
Three High Cards	2
Two High Cards	3
Inside Straight	1
Three to a Straight Flush w/gap	2
One High Card	4
Mixed Low Cards	5

Start at the top and work down until you find the first
draw that fits your hand and use it.

If you compare the tables, you'll see that the number of cards to draw for a particular hand is the same regardless of which strategy you use.

The only difference is in the ranking of the hands to obtain the particular strategy's result you desire. *Generally, the Royal Strategy gives more importance to a hand with royal flush potential than the Optimum Strategy. Conversely, the Conservative Strategy gives less importance to the royal flush potential than the Optimum.*

Where the strategies disagree starts with whether or not to break ANY winning hand. For example, the Royal Strategy will ALWAYS break Jacks-or-Better or Two Pair to go for a 1 or 2 card draw for a Royal Flush. The Conservative Strategy will keep the winning hands and try to draw to them. The Optimum Strategy will look at the expected values of each draw and, in this case, would break the Jacks-or-Better, but would keep the Two Pair.

The Optimum Strategy

The Optimum Strategy presented on page 89 is representative of various ones described by other authors. The hands are ranked in descending order according to their decreasing expected value. We have included only 19 entries — most strategy tables list from 16 to 20 hands, but many also include the top five hands. These are extremely condensed and selective versions of the ultimate table of approximately 331,000 different types of hands that could be dealt. One major manufacturer has over 200 entries in calculating its percentages. For example, we list an "open-end straight w/ 3 high cards" as ranking higher than a "low pair." The ultimate table would include the following:

Four to open-end straight w/ 3 high cards
Low Pair
Four to an open-end straight w/ 2 high cards
Four to an open-end straight w/ 1 high card
Three to a straight flush w/ 1 high card
Four to an open-end straight w/ 0 high cards

You can see that three cards to a straight flush could have a higher expected value than four to an open-end straight if the straight flush deal includes one high card. When you condense the table, such errors cannot be avoided. However, the differences in expected value are so minimal in long-term probability that they can be ignored also in short-term play.

Generally speaking, the optimum strategy is designed to approach, as nearly as possible, the programmed payback percentage of the machine. If used correctly — and the machine cooperates —

the Optimum Strategy should get the maximum return for the money invested.

The Royal Strategy

This strategy presented on page 90 is appropriate only for those who want the big bonus or jackpot regardless of the cost. It is for the aggressive player with a bankroll large enough to ignore the long-term probabilities, to ride out the losing streaks, and to catch up during the winning streaks. The royalist also ignores the expected values and pushes his luck to make the machine deal him the royal.

He is not interested in trying to make the machine pay its programmed percentage over long-term play. He wants more than a possible one percent for his investment. He wants the big jackpot and its bonus, if any.

Like the table for Conservative Strategy, this one has been condensed to 17 entries. However, the expected values of like hands have been distorted somewhat in favor of a draw to a royal flush at the possible expense of losing more probable payouts according to the Optimum method of play.

The royalist attitude is "nothing ventured, nothing gained." Sometimes he may get "reckless" and throw away a flush with four high cards, drawing one card to fill in the royal.

Example:

> A K Q J 6 of same suit (Discard the 6
> and hope for a 10 and an ordered royal.)
> A K Q 10 5 of same suit (Discard 5 and
> hope for a Jack)

He will almost always throw away a pat straight
with four cards to a Royal.

Example:

> A♡ K♡ Q♡ J♡ 10◇ (Discard 10◇
> to draw 10♡ for an ordered Royal.)
> K♣ Q♣ J♣ 10♣ 9♠ (Discard 9♠ to
> draw A♣)

These are the "exceptions" we mentioned
earlier. At this point, the royalist is veering off
course in an attempt to catch a shooting star. He
is plainly pressing his luck. If the progressive pot
or bonus is high enough, he considers the possible loss worth the risk. Sometimes the potential
win justifies the additional risk. As we stated
earlier, many strategists use a distorted Royal
Flush Strategy based on a trade-off of expected
value for a potentially larger payout.

The Conservative Strategy

The conservative strategy shown on page 91 is based on the assumption that the royal flush is practically impossible to hit and might as well be ignored. That appears to be an extremely pessimistic attitude. On the contrary, the conservative player's expectations are not inflated by dreams of instant wealth. Without such high aspirations, he will seldom be disappointed. He realistically — and patiently — plays for fun, and hopes for profit.

This method makes sense for "Staying Power,"* especially for the occasional player or a vacationer with limited time and, perhaps, limited funds. "Staying power" means making your money last as long as possible to conservatively increase your chances of winning by increasing your chances to play.

Actually, there are two types of conservative players — the uninformed or "ultra-conservative" and the knowledgeable or "cautious conservative."

By ignoring the royal flush, the ultra-conservative player can comfortably play less than

---

*Staying Power is a term coined by our publisher, John Gollehon, and represents the hallmark of his advice in *Winner Take All,* a book on dice scheduled for publication in mid-1992.

the maximum coins and still be delighted if he happens to hit it with only one to four coins played. Typically, he will begin play with one or two coins at a time to minimize his losses and will increase the number of coins up to the maximum if and when the machine starts to pay.** If he loses several hands in a row, he will drop back to one or two. He makes smaller bets for no regrets. In other words, "stretch a buck and stretch your luck!"

You might think that casinos do not like ultra-conservative players. On the contrary, the more jackpots hit for less than maximum coins played, the greater the "hold" percentage on the machine. The players using *Optimum* Strategy instead, however, are those who cut into casinos' profits.

The cautious conservative approach is to look for the machine with the highest payback for smaller wins, such as jacks-or-better. Also, you almost never throw away a winning hand. A few coins ready to drop are better than many coins that may not drop. A bet returned, if only for even money, is not lost and can be played again. It adds to your staying power.

Knowledgeable or cautious conservatives will avoid playing 5-8 progressive machines or those

---

**We never recommend playing less than the maximum number of coins. If playing the maximum number might put you in early jeopardy, then your stake is not large enough to begin with.

with wild cards because of the reduced payback for small winning hands. It doesn't make sense to contribute to a progressive jackpot you don't intend to win.

However, some ultra-conservatives feel that the wild cards increase the frequency of small wins which, therefore, justifies the reduced payout. We've seen players sit at a deuces wild, joker wild, or progressive machine and play for hours on five or ten dollars, playing only one or two coins at a time. If they hit anything larger than the original stake, they quit happy. If they eventually lose it all, they're content at having so much "fun" for a small price.

This attitude partially accounts for the casinos' trend to add more progressives and to add machines with more wild cards and more varied bonus paytables, even banks of mixed progressives. They expand that smorgasbord of choices and chances to fantastic limits. Progressive jackpots and wild and crazy machines are gradually replacing some straight video poker types in much the same way that video poker keeps edging out regular slot machines. Casinos will always offer the customers the games they want to play.

We purchased (for analysis) a "guaranteed winning system" based on the double-up method (not to be confused with Double Up machines). You start with four coins and play one at a time placing your winnings, if any, in a cup. Once you have lost all four coins, you increase your bet to two coins at a time. If you lose these, you increase your bet to three at a time; after losing these you increase, not to four, but to five at a time. When you win, depending on the amount you have lost, you go back to the lower number if you are still behind or start over with one coin if you are even or ahead. All coins won are put in a bucket and not played for any reason. The author of this system guarantees you will be ahead after playing out your $10 stake.

His system was outlined in nine 8½ by 11 pages with oversized double-spaced type at a cost of $30. It was recommended only for straight video poker machines which return a bet for jacks-or-better. The advertisement states, "If you ever have a losing trip you can return it for a full and prompt refund." Refund is good for six months.

Since the system was supposed to show a profit on a $10 roll of quarters, we tried it on three different machines and lost the $10 each time without a profit. We said, "Forget it." We also forgot to return it for a refund, since we wanted to include our results here. The cost of the system and the money lost testing it weren't worth it. In our opinion, it is a good example of someone who may be making more money "selling" the system than "using" it.

Unlike the ultra-conservative, the above system is based on increasing your bet when you're losing and decreasing it when you win. Apparently, it discounts the possibility of such a thing as a winning streak.

As any experienced gambler knows (or *should* know), you never press your losses. It's a sure road to defeat. The wise gambler, whether playing video poker, or dice, or any other game of chance, increases his bets only when he's winning, and ahead. He lays back on his betting, or quits, if he's losing.

Either conservative approach is all right if you ignore the royal flush and can be happy just playing for fun or for a small win. However, *if you're the conservative type, we suggest you play only nickel or quarter machines. The half-dollar and dollar types can gobble up a sizable stake in a very short time, regardless of whether you are cautious or not.*

LET'S MAKE IT VERY CLEAR THAT WE DO NOT RECOMMEND THE CONSERVATIVE STRATEGY FOR THE SERIOUS PLAYER. FURTHER, WE DO NOT RECOMMEND PLAYING LESS THAN THE MAXIMUM COINS TO WIN THE ROYAL, REGARDLESS OF THE TYPE OF MACHINE — STRAIGHT POKER, BONUS

POKER, PROGRESSIVE, OR WILD-CARD TYPE.

Whatever strategy you choose, we offer some do's and don'ts for your play:

1. ALWAYS PLAY THE MAXIMUM COINS. You are only throwing away the bonus money if you don't. Who knows, you might be the lucky one to hit the royal flush, regardless of the strategy you're using.

2. If you can't afford to play maximum coins, you can't afford to play. Go see a show instead.

3. If you're playing a dollar machine, and five coins (the max) is too much for you, drop down to a quarter machine. Likewise, if you are playing a quarter machine, and five coins is still too much for you, look for a nickel machine. There are still a few available, but only in Nevada. Atlantic City casino owners look down their noses at nickels. If you're stuck at a machine that's too expensive for you, regardless of where you are, stop.

4. Don't draw on hunches. Your feeling has no effect on the machine. If you think you're "psychic," go to the craps table; the overall odds can be better.

5. Never keep a "kicker." You are not playing against anyone else. You are playing against the odds. Note: A "kicker" is usually a high-ranking card held in addition to a pair.

Whether you are an Optimum, Royal, or Conservative player, always try to be optimistic. If not, there is no reason to play at all. Bon voyage on your "star trek."

CHAPTER 5

Managing Your Money

Video Poker is entertaining only as long as your funds last. It's not that much fun watching *other* people play. Few players are wealthy enough to feed the machines indiscriminately — to use the Royal Flush Strategy for the ultimate thrill at all costs. They're only trading their "jack" for a "jackpot." This section may interest them only if they must report their win to the Internal

Revenue Service and try to prove their losses equal their gains.

On the other hand, most players want their "play money" to last as long as their allotted "play time," and if they're lucky, they will turn it into substantial funds for other purposes. **Above all, a player must remember not to lose more than he can afford.** We hope these tips will help you to be **"cost** conscious" and avoid a **"cost** conscience" that will haunt you later.

Develop Discipline.

Developing discipline is the most important factor in avoiding the pitfalls of playing video poker that we have discussed in another chapter. Professional gamblers have to develop discipline, otherwise they soon become professional losers. If you plan to play frequently (one or more times a week) or as a tourist (every day of your trip), you need to set limits on both time and money. However, setting limits is futile unless you stick to them. It takes will power to resist the temptation to exceed your physical endurance and your financial resources when playing video poker.

Use Your Will Power.

If you must develop a habit playing video poker, let that habit be exercising your will power, and not becoming a habitual loser. There is no such thing as a "habitual winner." There are only occasional winners at this game or any other gambling activity.

If you have strong will power, great! But be careful. Video poker may take it to the limit. If you're lacking in will power, don't go alone. Take along a trusted relative or friend as your **"designated monitor" (DM)**. Tell your DM what limits you have set so that he or she can remind you when you're about to exceed them. The best DM is someone who does not particularly enjoy video poker or someone with great will power. Avoid playing with anyone who is less disciplined than yourself. Don't let another "blind-luck" player lead you down a "blind-luck" alley.

"Safety in numbers" is also a good axiom to follow. The larger your party the better. You're less likely to stay too long at a cold machine or keep buying more change if your friends are waiting to go to dinner or to go home. You'll feel guilty if they're standing behind you waiting for you to give up. On the other hand, if you're winning, it's more fun when there's someone to share your joy and to cheer for you. Ask the most disciplined person in your party to act as the designated monitor and *pay attention when he says it is time to stop.*

Set time limits and make them realistic.

Decide before you leave the house or hotel room how long you have to play. One to four hours at a time is enough. If you play longer than that, you'll get tired. Any game that lasts longer than four hours becomes "work." Work isn't fun, it's tiresome. "Just a little longer" is often the preface to "I should have quit when I was ahead."

Whether you play a progressive machine, prefer straight poker with a 6-9 paytable, or decide to try your luck at the wild card types, don't try to beat the clock. Wear or carry a watch. Remember, there are no clocks in casinos.

If you're playing alone, consult your watch frequently. You'd be surprised how quickly the time passes when you're watching that screen and concentrating on the cards.

If you're not alone, ask your DM or friends to check with you every 20 to 30 minutes in case you are ready to cut a losing streak short or, better yet, to quit a winner. Every time you do either of these two when prompted, you may gradually learn to do so on your own volition. You will learn to exercise your own will power. Let the power be with you.

Set cash limits and stick to them.

First, divide your total poker stake proportionately for the number and length of your playing sessions. Take only enough money with you to cover a single session of play.

Some strategists have calculated the cost per hour for trying to win the jackpot. Their figures are usually based on the assumption that you also play back the coins that are dropped. For instance, Wong estimates that a 5-8 quarter progressive in Nevada will cost $35 per hour if you play 500 hands per hour which is practically impossible as we have explained in the section on progressive teams. By his calculations, you will feed in $625 worth of quarters per hour playing five coins each hand, and the machine will pay out $590 of that amount. Don't count on that kind of return.

Also, according to Wong, you should average one royal flush every 62 hours at that rate, but he includes the disclaimer that you may not hit one at all. Of course, you might hit a royal on the first few hands or in the first hour. But don't count on that either. However, we doubt that you could play for 62 hours straight, especially at that fast a rate, nor do we recommend that you even attempt to do so. The faster you play the faster you pay! Why rush through something you enjoy?

Would you rush through a gourmet dinner? Would you rush through a relaxing round of golf? It's the same thing at the video poker machines. Relax, and enjoy yourself.

After you've apportioned your funds, take only the amount allotted for a single session. If you lose it, you won't lose the other sessions' allotment as well. The object is to stretch your funds over the expected number of playing periods. If you have to end one early, perhaps the next one will turn out better and you'll have part of your stake left at the end of your time — maybe you'll even win enough for that cruise, new TV, or paying off the car loan. You name it. It's always a good idea to set a concrete goal or incentive to save your winnings.

When your stake for each session is gone, even if your time is not, that session is over. If you have to wait for someone else, treat yourself to a piece of pie, visit the gift shop, see a movie, or bowl a game — any distraction to avoid being tempted to press your luck!

We can not stress this point enough. We have talked to many people who, when asked if they enjoyed their visit to Las Vegas, replied, "Yes, but it was one or two days too long because my cash ran out."

Don't play back your winnings.

You can interpret this tip two ways. First, play out your original stake and keep the machine pay-out in a separate "winnings" fund to keep track of your net wins and losses over the long run or group of play periods. This method will also allow you to keep track of the payback percentages of the machine you are playing. When a roll of quarters has been played, count up the "win-nings" in the tray. See if the payback is 95%, 100% or hopefully... 125% or more!

Second, you play back the coins paid at each session unless you are substantially ahead at any given moment, enough to justify quitting while you're ahead. Either way, if you hit a royal, "squirrel" it away. If you hit four-of-a-kind several times or a straight flush (except on certain wild card machines), that is a substantial amount — enough to cash in and stash in your "winnings" pocket. Any win that is hand-paid by an attendant should definitely be put away.

Cash out your credits frequently.

There are still machines at various locations that drop the coins with each win. However, most of the newer machines are credit types that accumulate all the wins until you push the "cash out" or "collect" button. There are several schools of thought on frequent cash-out. Some players never let the credits accumulate and never play them without cashing out to reinsert for each play. This method is slower and makes your money seem to last longer. Others play them as they accumulate, seldom inserting more coins when there are credits to play. Still others never play the credits; they let them add up and cash out only when they are ready to quit ahead, quit even, or have played their whole stake and all the credits as well and are broke. That's the problem with credits — it's too easy to play them all back before you realize how fast that total is approaching zero.

When playing a credit machine, don't mix your method of play. It is too easy to forget your credits if you do. Bradley Davis gives good advice in *Mastering Joker Wild Video Poker*:

> "If you play with credits, stick to play-
> ing credits; If you play with cash, then
> stick to playing cash."

Either way you play, don't forget to cash out before you leave the machine.

There is another advantage to frequent collection of credits. In cases of power failure, not all casinos have backup power enough to keep the machines going. On one occasion we and several players around us had built up credits that we couldn't afford to walk away from when a storm blacked out the entire casino. We sat for one and a half hours before power was restored so we could collect and leave. It's no fun being kept in the dark.

Don't carry checkbooks or automatic teller and credit cards into the casino.

Most casinos have the quick cash ATM's and credit card machines for customers to use. The temptation to replenish a lost stake may be too great to resist. Besides, the service charge for using the ATM's, at least in Nevada, is double if used in a casino rather than at a bank or other remote station. Also, the charge for cash advances on credit cards can be pretty steep, not to mention the interest rate on your monthly bill.

It is never a good idea to go in debt to gamble. If you apply for credit at the casino cashier's cage, there may not be an interest charge for your markers, but they do have to be repaid. Repayment of a gambling debt is very distasteful because there is seldom anything concrete to show for it. It becomes a reminder of a lack of discipline, and no one likes to be reminded of that.

You may want to obtain approval for cashing checks at your favorite casino in lieu of carrying a lot of cash in your purse or wallet. That's your choice. Just be careful that your will power is strong enough to avoid spending the mortgage or grocery money from your checking account for gambling.

Quit when you're ahead.

We can't emphasize this rule enough. It's the most difficult to follow. Having money left at the end of your allotted time is the ideal situation. Never stretch a playing session because you haven't spent all your stake. Add it to your "winnings" to balance out the sessions that were less productive. *Moderation is the key.*

Keep sessions short, even if you find a hot machine. A hot machine can turn cold before you realize it's playing *you* instead of vice versa. Don't let the machine capture your imagination and your self-control. Stay in charge!

Becoming a disciplined video poker player may not be easy at first, but later you'll appreciate the ability to enjoy the game without suffering from "slotaholic hangover," better known as "excessive loss syndrome." Always play for entertainment. Any other reason could be dangerous to your pocketbook and your peace of mind.

Keep records of wins and losses.

Keeping a track record of your gambling is not much fun, we admit. However, it can be very important if you hit a few royals, especially those $1,200 or more, which are reported to the Internal Revenue Service (IRS) by the casino. Winnings are income and taxable. For such wins you must produce appropriate identification and sign a W2G form before being paid.

Casinos don't like all the paperwork either. Unfortunately, it's the law. Uncle Sam wants his share of your wealth. That's one reason some casinos set the quarter bonus jackpots for royals at just under $1,200. Incidentally, there are considerably more royals hit on quarter poker than any other denomination probably because they are played more often.

You will, of course, want to deduct all your gambling losses as well as be able to prove them in case of an IRS inquiry or audit. You may only deduct losses up to the amount you report as won, and only for that year. Gambling losses may not be used to reduce taxes on other income. Keeping good records is the key.

You might carry a pocket calendar and record your "cash flow" daily, that is, amounts both won and lost. A small pocket notebook would probably allow more detail such as place, time, type of machine, etc. We included a blank form in *Slot Machine Mania* that is reproduced at the end of this section which you may use as an example. If well kept, the data should satisfy the IRS, but check with your accountant to be sure.

Your notes could be even more valuable to you as they reveal your playing habits, your most successful or most disappointing sessions, and even patterns that you may want to avoid or repeat. You may discover that your best results are on certain days of the week, on a specific type of machine, at a particular casino or other place, or even at the same hours of the day. You may even note the particular "strategy" employed each time to see which one works best for you. Note also if your strategy of play was consistent or erratic. Did you switch from Optimum to Royal or Conservative, etc.?

Develop a list of abbreviations to facilitate your entries. For instance:

      Places could be:
      TM   = Taj Mahal
      CC   = Circus Circus
      ST   = Sam's Town
      EX   = Excalibur
      GN   = Golden Nugget
      CT   = Caesars Tahoe

Machines could be
    S   = Straight poker
    SP   = Straight progressive
    DW = Deuces Wild
    JP   = Joker Poker
    JPP = Joker Poker Progressive
    DJW = Deuces-Joker Wild

Record also names of friends who accompanied you and can verify your presence, or casino employee's names if you are a regular customer.

Keeping your video poker diary or journal is a habit we encourage. The extent and style can be your own. Make it as elaborate or as simple as you wish. It may require some discipline to keep it up to date, but it will be easier than trying to fill in all the blanks later. Details of big jackpots remain sharp and clear, but losses seem to become foggy rather fast. Both are important to establish the cumulative totals on your "profit and loss statement."

Another way to keep track, if you are a member of a "Player Club," is to ask the casino for a print-out of your account's activity. Some people have used these as loss statements for their taxes.

By the way, keep all canceled checks written at the casinos, ATM receipts, and credit card bills as "proof of poker" — to lend credibility to your calendar of events. Incidentally, we overheard one player asking for a receipt for $100 in quarters. He said that Binion's Horseshoe gives receipts for purchases of $100 or more in coins. That sounds like a policy all casinos should adopt. The steady customers would appreciate it.

We hope your fortune and fun outweigh the effort spent recording their history. May you have many super jackpots to report and, ideally, that even exceed your losses.

DATE	TIME	PLACE	MACHINE TYPE	MACHINE NO.	AMOUNT SPENT	AMOUNT WON	NET LOSS	NET GAIN	WITNESSES/ COMMENTS

This chart is suitable for photo-copying

CHAPTER 6

Perks And Perils

To keep up with player demands, casinos continue to put more slots and video poker machines on the floor. Why buck the trend! They have found out its time to give credit where credit is due. That is, they have learned to "grow with the flow" of little spenders as well as big spenders, occasional players as well as frequent players and, most of all, locals as well as tourists. Promotional gimmicks to attract players have attained a sophistication that rivals the plastic credit card explosion. But just as the misuse of credit cards has led to the downfall of many a compulsive shopper, so has the proliferation of slots and video poker apparently contributed to unwise spending and in some cases to compulsive behavior.

Let's examine these two important aspects of gambling in more detail. We hope that as an informed player you will enjoy the perks and avoid the perils.

Player Clubs

Video poker and slots continue to become more efficient and productive with less risk of being prey to slot cheats, primarily due to the advances in microprocessor and video technology. With all the casinos competing for players, these advances also enable them to offer incentives such as larger jackpots and bonuses through "slot clubs," the more common name for "player tracking systems." Slot clubs are now the most prevalent form of "perk" used to track and reward slot and video players.

Historically, casinos were reluctant to institute computerized casino slot systems. When casino slot returns lagged behind other casino game revenues, slot tracking systems were not considered to be "cost effective." However, when slot revenues began to surpass those of table games, casinos and manufacturers took a closer look at the slots and ways of making them even more attractive to the average player as well as the high rollers. Computerized slot monitoring and player tracking systems were the only logical method of identifying and rewarding those responsible for their major profit item.

Electronic Data Technologies (EDT), a subsidiary of IGT, was the innovator with its "Player Club" system.* Although Bally Manufacturing and several other manufacturers developed slot accounting systems, the EDT system with its Player Club has found worldwide acceptance in the gaming industry.

Players are invited to join the club and accumulate bonus points by inserting their club card (or cards for playing multiple machines) in the card reader slot on each machine. The reader is either a box attached to the side of the machine or a special slot built into the new machines. Accumulated bonus points can be redeemed for a variety of gifts or services and, in some casinos, for cash. Redemption values also differ greatly from club to club. A consistent point accumulation keeps

---

*Co-author, Dwight Crevelt, at the age of 17, worked on development of a table-game monitoring system with Gamex Industries, a pioneer in electronically controlled slots. Simultaneously, he developed the first slot monitoring system. More recently, he worked with EDT on the development of their player tracking system.

players returning frequently — more than for special drawings for a big prize during a limited promotion.

When you insert your club card into the reader or machine, the display will greet you. For instance: "Hello, Joy, glad you're here. Your point balance is 1000. Coins to next bonus point: 18." The number of coins needed to earn the next bonus point differs depending on the type of machine, denomination, place you are playing, and the point at which the previous player withdrew his card. He may have run out of money or had to leave when only a few more coins played would have earned the bonus point. The reader does not reset to the maximum coins per point when a card is removed. We have seen players hopping from machine to machine testing each reader to select those requiring only a few plays. These point chasers "can't see the forest for the trees." The bonus points are more important to them than the jackpot. They're chasing the wrong rainbow if they're looking for that pot of gold.

Most slot clubs are not exclusive with membership. You can join as many clubs at different casinos as you wish. It's not uncommon to see a player with a credit-card wallet or a key-chain full of club cards. There is no initiation fee to join. Don't worry, you'll pay later — everytime you play the machine, the casino gets its "take" —

with or without the card in the reader. One club, however, does require you to become "eligible" by winning a certain number of colored tokens that fall periodically with the coins won while playing. Guess they're trying to discourage the occasional or infrequent players. We were "turned off" by this "pseudo-exclusive" requirement.

It seems that more and more players prefer to play video poker instead of the regular slots. Due to this imbalance of "reel" slot play to video poker play, some clubs have set the number of coins needed to earn a bonus point on "reel" slots at less than that on video poker machines. In some casinos, the ratio is almost 2 to 1. Further, most of the newer slot machines seldom require more than three coins played to win the top jackpot, unlike many older machines that required four, five, six, and sometimes nine coins for the bonus jackpot. One casino has even modified its system to give players of regular slot machines extra pay-outs if they are using their club card.

Finally, player tracking systems enable casinos to identify the slot and video poker "high rollers." At last, these customers are being recognized and rewarded for their contributions (literally) to the industry. They are "comped," complimented that is, with free dinners, gifts, parties, and other perks — privileges formerly reserved for table-game high rollers. Club members often receive periodic newsletters, notices of special promotions and tournaments, and coupons for discounts in casino restaurants or shops.

Now that most major casinos have slot clubs, they must compete for members. They use innovative and unique attractions to entice potential players to join their clubs, such as free bonus points and/or gifts at registration and extra bonus points on birthdays or for bringing in new members. Club cards even become the key to discounts and bonus promotions at other games such as bingo and bowling.

Some clubs offer double bonus points or other special gifts such as T-shirts, mugs, candy, and fanny packs on certain days or months; some offer occasional cash bonuses for a royal flush, provided you have your card in the reader when it hits. For instance, Sam's Town Royal Flush Club gives a bonus jacket for the first royal you hit each year and other incentives for subsequent royals. One month it was a spin on an extra cash wheel; another month it was a free T-shirt. Most of their special drawings require club registration. One drawing awarded both cash and extra bonus points which could only be collected incrementally over a two-week or 30-day period. *In the door — collect the prize — put it in the machines!* Winners didn't like this "incremental" payout of such small "daily" prizes.

Caesars Tahoe enticed members to join and rewarded their Emperors Club winners in June 1991 with the following bonus payouts when maximum coins were wagered:

Hit	Win
Dollar Sequential Royal Flush	$100,000
Quarter Sequential Royal Flush	$ 25,000
Dollar Sequential Straight Flush	$ 4,000
Quarter Sequential Straight Flush	$ 1,000

Sequential Royal Flush (10,J,Q,K,A)
Sequential Straight Flush (2,3,4,5,6 or 6,5,4,3,2)

Caesars Tahoe also advertises "Certified Friendly" service and "Slot Player's Edge!" (What else is new?)

By contrast, the Gold Coast in Las Vegas, which boasts over 190,000 club members, gives points for coins won rather than coins played. The Gold Coast also has a continuous, progressive, extra-bonus feature that ties all quarter, half-dollar, and dollar video poker machines into one giant progressive jackpot for a heart royal flush in sequence (either direction) with maximum coins played. Since wild card machines are also linked to the progressive, it must be a true royal, no deuces or jokers. To be eligible for this bonus, you must be a club member and have your card inserted at the time the hearts line up, or you will be "heart broken."

According to Gary Hunter, Gold Coast Slot Manager, there are 1,300 to 1,400 machines tied into that progressive bonus. Sometimes it gets as high as $26,000 before it is hit. That's a healthy bonus. It sometimes builds for weeks before those hearts line up. No wonder more than 80 percent of their slots are video poker. Small wonder, also, that the Gold Coast is a favorite of local video poker enthusiasts.

Some players were suspicious of the slot clubs at first. A few we know still persist in their belief that the card in the reader prevents the machine from hitting the jackpot. Not so! The card reader has absolutely no connection to the program that selects the winning symbols on a slot or the deal on video poker.

Should you join these clubs if you play frequently? Certainly! Take all the freebies you can get for your "investment." However, to ensure that you get the proper perspective, here's an example of cloudy vision: A friend of ours in a local service club plays several times a week at a local bar and restaurant with slot club incentives. He boasted of redeeming bonus points for a TV, VCR, microwave, and several other prizes during one year's play. That's several thousand dollars worth of merchandise. When we asked him how much money he lost to "win" those gifts, he reluctantly admitted that he could have purchased every one several times over. He did have fun, though, and that's the important fact to remember. Playing video poker should be entertainment, not a living — at least for the player.

Tournaments

Many casinos continue to promote periodic slot tournaments designed with perks to attract tourists with big bucks to spend. On the other hand, the video poker tournaments occasionally scheduled seem to be small potatoes by comparison. Most of them are held weekly or monthly, but the prizes do not compare with the cash, cars, and trips in the slot tournaments. Video poker tournaments are usually "entry free"; eligibility to enter can be earned by reaching a specific number of bonus points on the club card through regular play in a given time (e.g. day, week, month, etc.)

Apparently, casinos don't need to offer big prizes in video poker tournaments to encourage "practice" play on the machines. They're busier than slots all the time.

Non-Club Promotions

For some reason, a few casinos have not instituted a player tracking system. They advertise that they have "looser slots" and more frequent jackpots due to savings in cost by not having slot systems. We don't believe that. We've played at most of them and haven't had any better results than at casinos with clubs. They bank on other ways to keep players coming in to make their daily "deposits" in the slots.

The most common method is registration for daily drawings for cash and prizes. Usually the daily prizes are small ($100 to $500), but these token prizes keep players nibbling at the hook. Locals often burn up gallons of gas traveling from casino to casino, battling the traffic and racing the clock to be present to win the daily prize. On the final drawing day, they jam the parking lots and pack the casino floor, hoping for their name or number to be announced as winner of the Cadillac or 25 grand or whatever the bait is dangling at the end of the hook. These casinos without clubs don't know if they have frequent paying customers or just thousands of "entrants" who contribute little or nothing to their profit line. One of the most popular with the locals is the "Car a Day in May" hosted by Palace Station in Las Vegas.

Double Incentives

Some casinos believe in buttering their bread on both sides with slot clubs *and* special drawings.

The Showboat in Las Vegas held a special drawing to attract members and players and gave away 40 Saturn automobiles in 40 days. Contestants did not have to be club members but had to register daily to be eligible for the drawings. Each registrant's name and social security number were entered into the computer, and he had to show a picture ID with each subsequent daily registration to prevent him from stuffing the drum. Members or not, they became a potential "customer of record," to receive future invitations in the mail to join their "officer's club."

Casinos are constantly criticized for being "unfair" with these "pseudo-lotteries" and try to find ways of ensuring maximum participation with a minimum of flak from losers. They would rather see several hundred thousand potential gamblers enter the door and the drawing than a few steady customers who win all the marbles. They want volume business. It's the numbers that count. (What the heck! While you're there, why not play a roll or two of coins. Another roll? Why not? Keep turning on that "candle" on the machine to summon a change person. That jackpot is ready to hit!)

Additional Perks

Most casinos offer many small perks or comps to their customers. Check to see if the casino where you are playing is offering any specials. Some require coupons; others give them when you hit a specific hand such as four 7's on video poker. We have listed a few of these below:

Free drinks — You can request coffee, juice, mineral water, plain soda, etc. We advise moderation on alcoholic drinks.

Fun Books or Coupons — These usually include discounts for the hotel's show and buffet. Some require out-of-state identification.

T-shirts, hats, fanny packs, key chains (you name it.)

Free pulls on special slots for a "fantastic" prize (trip, cash, car, etc.)

Free candy on certain holidays — chocolate bunnies on Easter, chocolate hearts on Valetine Day, etc.

The newest perk we have seen is being offered by the Tropicana Hotel in Las Vegas for table blackjack players. While it is not on video poker it is influenced by poker. It is their "Jackpot Blackjack" — a progressive jackpot when a player is dealt four red 5's. They also have a "Thursday's Pay Day On The Island" with numerous specials which includes a bonus for video poker players who get paid double for four 5's.

Whenever you can get a bonus above and beyond the basic paytable of a machine, take it; but be careful. Remember, nothing in life is really free.

Possible Addiction

Now that gambling is legal in some form or other in 48 states, compulsive gambling is becoming a national concern. Besides the casinos of New Jersey, Nevada, and South Dakota, there are many legal ways and places to gamble. Bingo is legal in 44 states. Lotteries are legal in more than thirty states, not to mention the Canadian and other foreign lotteries that also advertise and capture players in the United States. Poker parlors are popular in California. Off-track betting on horses and dogs has always been popular, legal or not, so more states are making it legal and taxable.

Soon the "Great American Pastime" may not be sports, but *betting* on sports and other games of chance, if it isn't already. According to Earl Ubell in *Parade* magazine, an estimated 290 billion dollars was spent on gambling in 1990. Of that figure, only about 21 billion was spent on lotteries. That leaves the biggest chunk spent on the other forms of gambling.

However, the different entities who deal with compulsive gambling have different estimates of how widespread it is. In 1990, *Parade* magazine surveyed men and women in the United States at random on their views about money. Two questions related to gambling were:

"Do you gamble with more money than you can afford to lose?

"Do you bet on something whenever you can?"
They projected the results of 900 respondents
(not a very large sample) to indicate that the two
percent who answered "almost always" to the two
questions represents 3.5 million adult compulsive
gamblers nationally. Also, of the 900 who
responded, 20 percent admitted that they gamble
recklessly "often." *Parade* then projected that 20
percent to represent 35 million adults who are
potential compulsive gamblers.

Compulsive gambling, according to Tom Cum-
mings, executive director of the Massachusetts
Council on Compulsive Gambling, is an "invisible illness" affecting about five percent of the
population. According to Dr. Robert Hunter, clin-
ical director of the compulsive gambling program
at Charter Hospital in Las Vegas, only three percent of the population are compulsive gamblers.
Whether three or five percent is correct, all agree
that it's a problem that needs serious attention.

Unfortunately, however, not enough assistance
is available to study the problem or to provide
counseling for those who recognize and seek help
to overcome their compulsion or illness, especially
in the areas where potential victims have the most
opportunity to become addicted. The Massachusetts lottery contributes more than $1 mil-
lion a year to their council to study and provide
treatment for compulsive gambling. By contrast,

the council on Compulsive Gambling of New Jersey receives only $185,000 from the state general fund and must raise additional funds through donations from the gaming industry.

Even worse, the Las Vegas Council on Compulsive Gambling receives no government funding. Lynn Waddell reported in the *Las Vegas Sun* that Harrah's (owners of Holiday Casino) is the only contributor to the Las Vegas council.

New Jersey, at least, recognizes the seriousness of the problem. The state requires casinos in Atlantic City to post signs reading: "Bet with your head not over it." They also post the 800 number of the council. Advertisements on television and radio drew 24,000 to the hotline calls in three months — December 1990 through February 1991.

In Las Vegas, only the Holiday Casino posts a number for compulsive gamblers to call. Consequently, the Las Vegas Council on Compulsive Gambling receives only about 15 to 20 calls per month. According to Tom Roche of the State Gaming Control Board, Nevada casinos deal with compulsive gamblers "more discreetly." The Golden Nugget and Mirage encourage players who are gambling excessively to take a break or eat lunch and sometimes give them other "comps." Harrah's Corporation offers free counseling for its employees who are compulsive gamblers. Also,

Caesars Palace will sometimes pay for its employees to receive treatment for their gambling addiction.

Employee gambling can be a serious problem. That's why some casinos prohibit their employees from playing in the casinos where they work. Besides, it discourages customers when they recognize a casino employee on break or off duty winning a big jackpot. It tends to make customers think the machines or games are "rigged."

Recent studies of compulsive gambling show a rather shocking trend that points to this simple, entertaining game of video poker as a potentially addictive and destructive mechanism. More subtle than drugs and alcohol, it sometimes leads to the same consequences of family and financial ruin and even criminal activity.

Further, as a natural adjunct to the increased social and financial freedom enjoyed by women, gambling is another privilege that is no longer reserved for men. Consequently, the dangers associated with gambling in general have become more prominent with the popularity of the game preferred by women, video poker.

A series of articles by Lynn Waddell in the *Las Vegas Sun* revealed some startling statistics on compulsive gambling. The typical video poker addict is a white, married woman, aged 30 to 40 who "sits entranced" at a machine from 7 to 25 hours at a time. She's not usually a tourist but a resident who can't pass up a machine at the grocery, drug store, or laundromat and who probably spends most of her spare time in her favorite casino.

Further, according to Dr. Hunter, before the advent of video poker, a Gamblers Anonymous meeting in 1985 would include perhaps only one woman. Now the women often outnumber the men. Dr. Hunter also stated that *95.5 percent of the women gamblers treated at Charter Hospital in Las Vegas played only video poker.*

Mary Lou Strachan, a former compulsive gambler, surveyed 52 women attendees of Gamblers Anonymous. Of the 52, 47 were addicted to video poker. Twenty-seven percent of those surveyed said that they had considered prostitution to support their habit but only 10 percent had actually done so. Strachan's survey also revealed that 87 percent of the women spent family savings, 76 percent obtained cash advances on credit cards, and 60 percent sold personal jewelry and other valuables to obtain cash for gambling. In debt from gambling, 69 percent had contemplated suicide and 23 percent had actually attempted it. (As a result of our own observation, we are not surprised by these shocking statistics.)

Another factor that the studies have revealed is that gambling addicts have a propensity for addiction as a result of hereditary and environmental influences. Many have a history of physical or sexual abuse, as well as drug, alcohol, or other addictive disorders — either personally or in their families. Many children whose parents are or were compulsive gamblers follow in their footsteps. Unfortunately, their predisposition is seldom discovered until they become adults and are already addicted. Of the women surveyed by Strachan, 42 percent had parents who gambled too much, 42 percent had alcoholic parents (not stated if these were the same ones), and 33 percent had suffered other addictions. Dr. Hunter agrees that "there seems to be a genetic connection." Perhaps researchers will eventually isolate a gene that is responsible for addictive behavior. We hope so.

Women are not the only victims, however; Strachan stated that her observations revealed that video poker was not necessarily "gender specific." She found that over 50 percent of the male members of Gamblers Anonymous are video poker addicts, also. Let's not give the ladies a bad rap. We've observed just as many men as women fascinated by the poker machines.

Why is video poker so addictive? Why are women so vulnerable? Dr. Hunter said that one reason may be that it is less intimidating and more socially acceptable than other forms of gambling. Further, he says that video poker meets all the fixating criteria. According to Waddell, experts say that those criteria are:

1. The ability to get immediate feedback.
2. The ability to increase time and money.
3. The false sense that the player can become good at it.
4. The ability to block out other activity.

The "instant gratification" and "immediate feedback" afforded by video poker hold the participants' attention without the suspense and tension of waiting for results as in bingo, sports betting, or the lottery. Setting his own pace, a player doesn't have to contend with a dealer or other players who may slow down the action or perhaps "rush" his decision to draw or stand as in table poker or blackjack.

Certainly, the immediate returns possible, whether miniscule or major, are definitely a factor for players seeking to double their money as well as their fun. Hitting occasional jackpots can be more addictive than constantly losing. The average player will willingly give up if he never wins, but winning "a little" feeds the greed and the need to win more and bigger amounts. Winning a large jackpot fires the imagination even more, and the potential addict works harder to repeat or exceed that big win.

The skill factor in video poker, insignificant as it may be in actual results, definitely lures the player into a *false* sense of control over the machine and the game. *You'll never become "proficient" at playing video poker.* The highs and lows in your bank account will prove that, at best, you will become an "average" player — it's the law of averages. The machine has the edge; its computer memory may not be as vast as the human brain, but it's definitely faster.

The "ability to blank out other activity" while sitting at a poker machine is admittedly one reason many men and women spend hours staring at that screen. They're escaping from other problems that become intolerable or that they can't solve. After all, it is an accepted fact that television is responsible for millions of couch potatoes. Add the fascination of a TV game to the other three criteria and you will understand why a steady diet of video poker can lead you into fantasyland.

Now that you are aware of the perils and pitfalls of trying to survive on a steady diet of video poker, we hope you'll avoid being trapped. As we have stated in the section on managing your money, moderation is the key to avoid entrapment by a "machine." If you have the slightest inclination toward addictive behavior of any kind, be very careful. LIMIT YOUR EXPOSURE, PLEASE.

Authors' Profile

Co-author Dwight Crevelt is a 20-year veteran of the engineering department at several slot machine manufacturers. He is currently a senior engineer on the technical staff at EDT, working in the Special Products Division. While at EDT, Dwight helped to design and engineer one of the casino's most complex pieces of equipment: The Player Tracking and Accounting System that is still in widespread use.

In fact, Dwight pioneered the concept of Slot Accounting Systems while working at Gamex in 1974. His original design was the first to be used in casinos.

Crevelt reached another benchmark in slot machine design several years ago when he developed the Memory Comparator, a device used by casinos to verify EPROMS in slot machines that tells the casino a jackpot is valid. (i.e. that the machine has not been tampered with.) This remarkable piece of equipment is still in use today.

The co-author, who was also the Director of Research at Mills-Jennings in the early 1980s, now is involved in much more than slot machine design and engineering. In addition to his present engineering duties at EDT, he is responsible for presenting new products to gaming regulatory agencies throughout the country, working as a liaison for the manufacturer.

Crevelt is called upon frequently as an expert witness in court hearings to report on the quality and performance of slot machines, and to help determine flaws or malfunctions in their design.

A Missouri native, Crevelt is also a member of the American Society of Naval Engineers, and a lobbyist for the Nevada Legislature. He was one of the first graduates to receive a degree in computer design and engineering from Iowa State University.

Crevelt's mother, Louise, who co-authored *Video Poker Mania,* and their original book, *Slot Machine Mania,* is a retired English instructor at the University of Nevada Las Vegas (UNLV), and remains an active enthusiast of slots. Her valued contribution to these works has made it possible for readers to understand the highly esoteric aspects of today's high-tech slot machines.

Bibliography

All About Slots and Video Poker, John Gollehon, G.P. Putnam's Sons, New York, N.Y., 1985

The Gambling Times Guide to Playing Games For Fun and Profit, Len Miller, Gambling Times Inc., Hollywood, California, 1983

Mastering Joker Wild Video Poker, Bradley Davis, Applied Technology Press, Aurora, Colorado, 1990

Slot Machine Mania, Dwight and Louise Crevelt, Gollehon Press, Inc., Grand Rapids Michigan, 1989

Winning Poker, David Sklansky, Prentice-Hall Inc., Englewood Cliffs, New Jersey, 1983

How To Win At Video Poker, David R. Gerhardt, Gerhardt Software, Madison Heights, Michigan, 1987

A Guide to Video Poker, Seattle Institute of Scientific Gaming, Seattle, Washington, 1982

Expert Video Poker for Las Vegas, Lenny Frome, Compu-Flyers, Las Vegas, Nevada, 1989

Beating the Poker Slot Machines, R. Carl Cohen, Philadelphia, Pennsylvania, 1981

Professional Video Poker, Stanford Wong, Pi Yee Press, La Jolla, California, 1988

Strategic Video Poker, computer program by Wendy Weiner, LWS Software, Havertown, Pennsylvania, 1990

Silberstang's Guide To Poker, Edwin Silberstang, Putnam Publishing Group, New York, New York, 1985

Video Poker Analyzer, computer program by Standford Wong, Pi Yee Press, La Jolla, California, 1991

"The Video Poker System that Wins Playing With a $10 Roll of Quarters," Walter Kemp, 1990

Las Vegas Sun Newspaper, selected articles

Las Vegas Review-Journal Newspaper, selected articles

"Centurian," Caesars Tahoe, Lake Tahoe, Nevada

Introduction to Probability Theory and Statistical Inference, Harold J. Larson, John Wiley & Sons, New York, New York, 1974

Poker Strategy and Winning Play, A. D. Livingston, J. B. Lippincott Company, Philadelphia, Pennsylvania, 1971

The Mathematics of Games and Gambling, Edward Packel, The Mathematical Association of America, 1981

State of Nevada Regulations: Nevada Gaming
Commission and State Gaming Control
Board, Carson City, Nevada

Gaming & Wagering Business, BMT Publica-
tions, New York, New York, Selected
Articles

"Nevada Gaming Abstract," State Gaming
Control Board, Carson City, Nevada

What's On In Las Vegas Magazine, Las
Vegas, Nevada

Parade, The Sunday Newspaper Magazine,
New York, NY

Why Gamble With Gambling Books?
Gollehon Is Your Best Bet!

Order three or more of these top-selling books and we'll send you a Four-Color Betting Strategy Card FREE, just like John Gollehon uses at all the games. Available only through this offer!

CONQUERING CASINO CRAPS, John Gollehon. From the basics to powerful strategies! 192 pages, $6.99

HOW TO AVOID CASINO TRAPS! John Alcamo. Play "defensively" and turn the tables! 160 pages, $6.99

HOW TO WIN! John Gollehon. New, winning strategies to beat craps, blackjack, roulette, and slots! 192 pages, $6.99

BEAT THE TRACK! Ada Kulleck. Play the thoroughbreds or harness horses and win with skill! 192 pages, $6.99

WHAT CASINOS DON'T WANT YOU TO KNOW, John Gollehon. Learn the six secrets of winning! 192 pages, $6.99

CASINO GAMES, John Gollehon. Clear and concise! ALL the rules for ALL the games! 256 pages, $7.99

THE BOOK CASINO MANAGERS FEAR THE MOST! Marvin Karlins. A new way to win! 256 pages, $7.99

COMMANDO CRAPS & BLACKJACK! John Gollehon. A gambling classic! With new strategies. 160 pages, $10.99

BUDGET GAMBLING, John Gollehon. Gambling's Bestseller! Bet little and win big! 256 pages, $14.99

HOW TO ORDER: Send check to Gollehon Press, Inc., 6157 28th St. SE, Grand Rapids, MI 49546. List the books you want on a piece of paper along with your name and address printed neatly. Add only $1 per book for shipping & handling. Orders usually ship within five days.

Here's how to get your own set of John Gollehon's personal Strategy Cards and save MONEY doing it!

The author's popular Strategy Cards have become the hottest cards on the market! The set retails for $12 in shops, but you can order the complete set by mail for only $9.95. Your cards go out within 48 hours and we pay the first-class postage!

BLACKJACK: Every player-hand and dealer up-card combination is listed, so you'll know exactly when to hit, stand, split, or double down. The Strategy Card does all the work!

CRAPS: All the payoffs for the bets you'll be making are listed so you can be sure you're getting all the winnings you deserve! A complete rundown for playing the game is also included.

VIDEO POKER: Follow a clever strategy to increase your chances of hitting a royal flush by 20 percent! The best paytables are listed, so you'll know exactly what machines to look for.

ROULETTE: A precise layout of the wheel is shown so that you can clock the dealer and predict the segment where the ball should land. See if you can beat the wheel with skill!

HOW TO ORDER:

Send check or money order for only $9.95 to: Gollehon Press, Inc., 6157 28th St. SE, Grand Rapids, MI 49546. Just write "Strategy Cards" on a piece of paper along with your name and address printed neatly.

Order your complete set today and start winning!